View here the Shadow whose Ingenious Hand
Hath drawne exact the Province Mary Land
Display'd her Glory in such Scænes of Witt
That those that read must fall in Love with it
For which his Labour hee deserves the praise
As well as Poets, doe the wreath of Bays.

Anno Do: 1666. Ætatis Suæ 28.   H.W.

GEORGE ALSOP, from the Portrait *in* the Original Edition of
1666.

Alsop's Maryland

A CHARACTER OF THE PROVINCE OF MARYLAND

BY

George Alsop

WITH
INTRODUCTION AND NOTES
BY

Newton D. Mereness, Ph.D.
ACTING PROFESSOR OF HISTORY AND ECONOMICS
IN THE COLLEGE OF CHARLESTON.
AUTHOR OF *Maryland as a Proprietary Province.*

HERITAGE BOOKS
2015

HERITAGE BOOKS

AN IMPRINT OF HERITAGE BOOKS, INC.

Books, CDs, and more—Worldwide

For our listing of thousands of titles see our website
at
www.HeritageBooks.com

A Facsimile Reprint
Published 2015 by
HERITAGE BOOKS, INC.
Publishing Division
5810 Ruatan Street
Berwyn Heights, Md. 20740

— Publisher's Notice —
In reprints such as this, it is often not possible to remove blemishes from
the original. We feel the contents of this book warrant its reissue despite
these blemishes and hope you will agree and read it with pleasure.

International Standard Book Numbers
Paperbound: 978-0-7884-1971-3
Clothbound: 978-0-7884-6138-5

INTRODUCTION

OF the few descriptions of Maryland written in the seventeenth century, this is decidedly the most pretentious. Its primeval savor, the peculiarity of its style, and its unique account of the mighty Susquehannas, together with its portrayal of the early white settlers of that province as a well-disposed people living under a well-ordered government in the midst of Nature's bountiful gifts, make it an enduring attraction to the curious reader; and when read in connection with other literature on the subject it is not without its value to the most serious student of our early history.

Only one month after the arrival of the colonists at St. Marys, in the year 1634, Father Andrew White, a Jesuit priest, wrote in Latin, and probably also in English, an account of the voyage, of the planting of the colony, and of what he had seen in the province. The next year, for the purpose of making this new possession attractive to all who could be persuaded to embark their fortunes in the New World, Lord Baltimore caused to be published in London a description probably prepared from Father White's account and from letters written by Governor Calvert and others. This was followed the next year by the publication in the same city of a more extended description of the riches of the province and with such additional information and directions as was thought might be of service to adventurers going thither to plant.

For the next twenty-five years the greatest need of the province was not so much glowing descriptions to attract colonists as it was prudence and skill in managing those already within its borders. For within that interval Claiborne and his men would submit only after being compelled to yield to superior force; the Jesuit priests made exorbitant claims for the canon law; Claiborne and Ingle, with their followers, kept the province in a state of insurrection for nearly two years; the Puritan commissioners seized the government and retained possession of it for four years; Fendall and his followers made an attempt to establish a commonwealth. From the rebel and the grumbler there went to England during these troublous times unfavorable accounts of the lord proprietor's government and tales of woe about the harsh treatment to which those were subjected who had gone there as indented servants. Hammond found occasion in the year 1656 to answer these charges in his *Leah and Rachel.*

But upon the return of stability to the home

government, with the Restoration of 1660, that which had been the chief cause of the disturbances in Maryland was removed, and the conditions seemed favorable for a new era of development. The population had up to this time increased to perhaps not more than six thousand, and it had become more and more exclusively engaged in the culture of tobacco. But now the lord proprietor sent out his son as governor, and both proprietor and governor were eager to attract more laborers, to encourage the growing of grain as well as the raising of stock, and to further the development of the resources of the province in every other possible way. To promote these ends it seems highly probable that Alsop was encouraged by the proprietor, together with such merchant adventurers as were interested in that part of the carrying trade, to write the description which we have in this little volume.

Our knowledge of this author is chiefly derived from what he has here written. He, the elder of two brothers, was born of obscure parentage in England in the year 1638. His childhood was therefore passed while his country was in the throes of a great civil war. In his youth he acquired a superficial book learning and a fondness for making verses. When not more than eighteen years of age he began to serve an apprenticeship to some trade in London, at which post he remained

for two years. At the age of twenty, in September,
1658, he embarked at Gravesend for Maryland
where he landed, as he says, after a five months'
dangerous passage. There, in Baltimore County,
he worked for four years for Mr. Thomas Stockett
as an indented servant. He became dangerously
ill soon after the expiration of this term of servitude. But he sufficiently recovered to return to
England and there complete the writing of his
description, "the major part of which," he tells
us, "was written in the intermitting time of his
sickness." This was published in 1666 when he
was only twenty-eight years of age. Of his
subsequent life nothing is known.

He was an ardent Royalist, bitter in his contempt of Cromwell and the Puritans, adhering
from his religious nature to the theory of the
divine right of kings, showing "an obedient
respect and reverence" for his parents, and
regarding the relation of master and servant as
natural and necessary as that of king and subject.
At the same time his little learning made him
verbose, bombastic, given to ridiculous extrava-
gance in style — even for his time — rather than
refined, cultured, accurate; and his acquaintance
with the disreputable places in London, together
with the low moral standard of the period of the
Restoration, made him vulgar rather than Puri-
tanical in his tastes. He admitted that he might

be wild and confused and thought the world "not very much out of the same trim."

In his letters written just before sailing, the only reason he gave for going to Maryland was that the world being in a heap of troubles and confusion he thought best to go out of it; and shortly after his arrival there he wrote that, had he known his yoke would be so easy as it then promised to be, he should have come much sooner rather than to have dwelt under the pressure of a rebellious and traitorous government as long as he had.

If these letters are genuine, he should be given some credit for the fact that what he wrote to his relatives and friends as his earlier impressions of the province are scarcely less in praise of it than what he wrote later for seemingly mercenary ends and advertising purposes. In one addressed to his father, for example, he tells of the wonderfully good living, contentment, and loyalty of the people, of the loving demeanor of the lord proprietor and the governor, of how the servants lived more like freemen than most mechanic apprentices in London and wanted for nothing that was necessary or convenient, of the variety of delightful woods, pleasant groves, lovely springs, spacious navigable rivers, the healthfulness of the climate, and the great numbers of deer and swine.

The man whom he served, in Maryland, the kind of labor he seems to have performed for him, the place where they lived, and the particular time at which he was there, must have contrib-uted much to his favorable impressions, to his opportunities for seeing the country as Nature made it, and especially to his knowledge of the Susquehanna Indians. This master, Mr. Thomas Stockett, was next to the eldest of four brothers who came to Maryland in the spring or summer of 1658 and settled in Baltimore County on what was then practically the border between the whites and the Indians. Each and all of these brothers — Lewis, Thomas, Francis, and Henry — were soon intrusted with the discharge of impor-tant public duties. Lewis was for a few years colonel and commander-in-chief of all the forces in the North and on the Isle of Kent. Francis was chosen a burgess of his county within less than a year after his arrival in the province. As a mem-ber of the assembly during the Fendall rebellion he held out for the lord proprietor until overcome by fear, and when that rebellion had been put down he asked for pardon. He was also appointed chirurgeon of a company sent to Susquehanna Fort to aid the Susquehanna Indians. Henry was a justice of the quorum in the court of his county.

But Thomas, in whom we are here more especially interested, was the greatest public servant of them all. He was a burgess of Baltimore County and a justice of the quorum in the court of the same county from 1661 to 1664. In 1663 he served on a committee of the lower house of assembly to consider Indian affairs. The year following he was named by that house as a fit man to treat with the Susquehanna Indians. One of the terms of a treaty with those Indians required that none of them should come farther among the English plantations than where Captain Thomas Stockett or Jacob Clauson lived without first procuring a pass from one of those gentlemen. There is no trace of the other three brothers in Maryland after the year 1666 and according to tradition they moved into Anne Arundel County about that year and a little later returned to England. But Thomas, after moving with his brothers into Anne Arundel County, served there as sheriff, and a part of the time as deputy surveyor-general of the province, until his death in April, 1671. If we may judge from the expressions in his will he was a very pious man. Be that as it may, he left one son, Thomas, and from his marriage with Mary Sprigg, of a prominent Maryland family, and a subsequent marriage with Damarris Welch, the Stocketts of Maryland, Kentucky, Pennsylvania, New York, and New Jersey are descended.

In the following pages Alsop makes only favorable mention of the treatment he received on the Stockett estate; leads one to think that he labored there as an artisan, or as an assistant in trade with the Indians, or both; tells us that at one time his master had in his house "four score venisons besides plenty of other provisions to serve his family nine months;" and after serving him four years, says he somewhat wished he had yet another four to serve. It seems highly probable, therefore, that our author, while an indented servant in Maryland, fared far better than those serving less bountiful and less humane masters, living in what were more exclusively the tobacco districts, and experiencing the drudgery of growing that plant and preparing it for the market.

Again, up to the time of Alsop's arrival in the province the culture of tobacco was still quite profitable, and when he returned to England the planters of Maryland had had only their first experience of the hardships resulting from a fall in the price of that commodity — about threepence per pound in the year 1649, but a drug on the market by the time this book was published in 1666. Furthermore, the easy suppression of the Fendall rebellion about a year after he came was followed by a few years in which there was a large measure of settled and submissive feeling toward the government. But serious disagreement between the two houses of assembly arose in the year 1666 over the tobacco question, the governor saw fit to allow three years to pass before calling another session of that body, and then the lower house came forward with its grievances.

Some of the conditions described in this book are consequently quite in contrast with the real conditions for the year in which it was published. Some of them are also far more flattering than those described in the account given by Dankers and Sluyters — two Labadist travelers — thirteen years later, where we are told that servants poorly fed and poorly housed, after wearing themselves down the whole day by working in tobacco, had yet to grind and pound the grain, usually maize, for their godless and crafty masters as well as for themselves. But these gentlemen, like Alsop, spoke of the fertility of the soil, the goodness of the timber, and the large quantities of fish; were greatly impressed with the vast numbers of water fowl, and said that with the proper application to the growing of other products than tobacco the inhabitants of Maryland might have everything for the support of life in abundance.

The original of this little publication is a small volume of 140 pages, the printed matter on each full one being only $2\frac{3}{4}$ x $4\frac{3}{4}$ inches. There are only a few of these now in this country. In the Lenox

Library, New York, are the Lenox copy and the
Bancroft copy. The latter has long been imperfect in text and deficient in both portrait and
map. The former had a few imperfect pages and
was deficient in portrait; but the imperfect pages
have been replaced by good ones from the Bancroft copy and a portrait for it has been taken
from a copy of Gowans's reprint which is a photo-
lithograph of the original; a second portrait, less
like the original, has also been added. Of three
other quite perfect copies known to be in this
country, one is in the John Carter Brown Library,
one was once in the collection of Henry C. Murphy,
and one in that of Samuel L. M. Barlow.

A reprint from the original, edited by John
Gilmary Shea, was published by William Gowans
in New York in 1869; and eleven years later this
reprint was reissued in Baltimore by The Maryland
Historical Society as Fund Publication, No. 15.

Newton D. Mereness.

ALSOP'S MARYLAND

LONDON : PETER DRING
1666

Title-page, portrait (frontispiece), and map reprinted from a copy of the original edition in
the John Carter Brown Library, Providence, R. I.   Text reprinted from the
"Lenox copy," in the Lenox
Library, New York City.

A
CHARACTER
Of the PROVINCE of
MARY-LAND,

Wherein is Described in four diſtinct
Parts, (*Viz.*)

I. The *Scituation*, and plenty of the Province.

II. The *Laws*, *Cuſtoms*, and natural Demeanor of the *Inhabitant*.

III. The *worſt* and *beſt Uſage* of a Mary-
Land *Servant*, opened in view.

IV. The *Traffique*, and vendable Commodities
of the Countrey.

ALSO

A ſmall *Treatiſe* on the wilde and
naked INDIANS (or *Suſquehanokes*)
of *Mary-Land*, their Cuſtoms, Manners, Abſurdities, & Religion.

Together with a Collection of Hiſto-
rical LETTERS.

By GEORGE ALSOP.

London, Printed by T. J. for Peter Dring,
at the ſign of the Sun in the Poultrey: 1666.

To the Right Honorable

Cæcilius Lord Baltemore,

Absolute Lord and Proprietary of the Provinces of

Mary-Land and *Avalon* in *America.**

My Lord,

I Have adventured on your Lordships acceptance by guess; if presumption has led me into an Error that deserves correction, I heartily beg Indempnity, and resolve to repent soundly for it, and do so no more.   What I present I know to be true, *Experientia docet;* It being an infallible Maxim, *That there is no Globe like the occular and experimental view of a Countrey.*   And had not Fate by a necessary imployment, confin'd me within the narrow walks of a four years Servitude, and by degrees led me through the most intricate and dubious paths of this Countrey, by a commanding and undeniable Enjoyment, I could not, nor should I ever have undertaken to have written a line of this nature.

---

*George Calvert, first Lord Baltimore, was at one time a chief secretary of state under James I. and from that monarch received, in the year 1623, a grant of the province of Avalon, the southeastern peninsula of Newfoundland. Finding the soil and the climate of Avalon unsuitable for the planting of a colony, he visited Virginia in the year 1629 and upon his return to England applied for a new grant, with the result that he was about to secure that of Maryland when death overtook him in April, 1632. After a delay of only two months it was issued to his eldest son, Cecilius, who thereupon became the lord proprietor of both Maryland and Avalon and as such continued until his death in 1675.

If I have wrote or composed any thing that's wilde and confused, it is because I am so my self, and the world, as far as I can perceive, is not much out of the same trim; therefore I resolve, if I am brought to the Bar of *Common Law* for any thing I have done here, to plead *Non compos mentis,* to save my Bacon.

There is an old Saying in English, *He must rise betimes that would please every one.* And I am afraid I have lain so long a bed, that I think I shall please no body; if it must be so, I cannot help it. But as *Feltham* * in his *Resolves* says, *In things that must be, 'tis good to be resolute ;* And therefore what Destiny has ordained, I am resolved to wink, and stand to it. So leaving your Honour to more serious meditations, I subscribe my self,

> *My Lord,*
>> Your Lordship most
>>> Humble Servant,
>>>> *George Alsop.*

---

* Owen Felltham (or Feltham), when a youth of eighteen, wrote a small volume of essays entitled, *Resolves, Divine, Moral and Political.* They were extremely popular during the seventeenth century. The first edition, published in 1628, was followed by a second in the same year, nine more before the year 1700, and several since. An edition, edited by Alexander Young, appeared in this country in 1832.

To all the Merchant Adventurers for *MARY-LAND*, together with those Commanders of Ships that saile into that Province.

Sɪʀѕ,

Yᴏᴜ *are both Adventurers, the one of Estate, the other of Life : I could tell you I am an Adventurer too, if I durst presume to come into your Company. I have ventured to come abroad in Print, and if I should be laughed at for my good meaning, it would so break the credit of my Understanding, that I should never dare to shew my face upon the Exchange oꝛ (conceited) Wits again.*

This dish of Discourse was intended for you at first, but it was manners to let my Lord have the first cut, the Pye being his own. I beseech you accept of the matter as 'tis drest, only to stay your stomachs, and I'le promise you the next shall be better done. 'Tis all as I can serve you in at present, and it may be questionable whether I have served you in this or no. Here I present you with **A Character** *of* **Mary-Land,** *it may be you will say 'tis weakly done, if you do I cannot help it, 'tis as well as I could do it, considering the several Obstacles that like blocks were thrown in my way to hinder my proceeding: The major part thereof was written in the intermitting time of my sickness, therefore I hope the afflicting weakness of my Microcosm may plead a just excuse for some imperfections of my*

*ven.   I protest what I have writ is from an experimen-
tal knowledge of the Country, and not from any
imaginary supposition.   If I am blamed for what I
have done too much, it is the first, and I will irrevocably promise it shall be the last.   There's a Maxim
upon Tryals at Assizes, That if a thief be taken
upon the first fault, if it be not to hainous, they only
burn him in the hand and let him go: *   So I desire
you to do by me, if you find any thing that bears a
criminal absurdity in it, only burn me for my first
fact and let me go.   But I am affraid I have kept you
too long in the Entry, I shall desire you therefore to
come in and sit down.*

G. Alsop.

---

* Burning in the hand was not so much a punishment as it was a
mark on those who, found guilty of felony, pleaded the benefit of
clergy, which they were allowed to do but once.

PREFACE

READER.

THE Reason why I appear in this place is, lest the general Reader should conclude I have nothing to say for my self; and truly he's in the right on't, for I have but little to say (for my self) at this time: For I have had so large a Journey, and so heavy a Burden to bring *Mary-Land* into *England*, that I am almost out of breath: I'le promise you after I am come to my self, you shall hear more of me. Good Reader, because you see me make a brief Apologetical excuse for my self, don't judge me; for I am so self-conceited of my own merits, that I almost think I want none. *De Lege non judicandum ex solâ linea*, saith the Civilian; We must not pass judgement upon a Law by one line: And because we see but a small Bush at a Tavern door, conclude there is no Canary. For as in our vulgar Resolves 'tis said, *A good face needs no Band, and an ill one deserves none:* So the French Proverb sayes, *Bon Vien il n'a faut point de Ensigne,* Good Wine needs no Bush. I suppose by this time some of my speculative observers have judged me vainglorious; but if they did but rightly consider me, they would not be so censorious. For I dwell so far from Neighbors, that if I do not praise my self, no body else will: And since I am left alone, I am resolved to summon the *Magna Charta* of Fowles to the Bar for my excuse, and by their irrevocable Statutes plead my discharge, *For its an ill Bird will befoule her own Nest:* Besides, I have a thousand *Billings-gate* * Collegians that will give in their testimony, *That they never knew a Fish-woman cry stinking Fish.* Thus leaving the Nostrils of the Citizens Wives to demonstrate what they please as to that, and thee (Good Reader) to say what thou wilt, I bid thee Farewel.

Geo. Alsop.

---

* Billingsgate, a little below London bridge, is the great fish market of that city. The language spoken there, especially by women, has made the word a synonym of vulgar and foul expressions.

AUTHOR

BOOK.

WHen first *Apollo* got my brain with Childe,
    He made large promise never to beguile,
But like an honest Father, he would keep
Whatever Issue from my Brain did creep:
With that I gave consent, and up he threw
Me on a Bench, and strangely he did do;
Then every week he daily came to see
How his new Physick still did work with me.
And when he did perceive he'd don the feat,
Like an unworthy man he made retreat,
Left me in desolation, and where none
Compassionated when they heard me groan.
What could he judge the Parish then would think,
To see me fair, his Brat as black as Ink?
If they had eyes, they'd swear I were no Nun,
But got with Child by some black *Africk* Son,
And so condemn me for my Fornication,
To beat them Hemp to stifle half the Nation.
Well, since 'tis so, I'le alter this base Fate,
And lay his Bastard at some Noble's Gate;
Withdraw my self from Beadles, and from such,
Who would give twelve pence I were in their clutch:

Then, who can tell? this Child which I do hide,
May be in time a Small-beer Col'nel *Pride.**
But while I talk, my business it is dumb,
I must lay double-clothes unto thy Bum,
Then lap thee warm, and to the world commit
The Bastard Off-spring of a New-born wit.
Farewel, poor Brat, thou in a monstrous World,
In swadling bands, thus up and down art hurl'd;
There to receive what Destiny doth contrive,
Either to perish, or be sav'd alive.
Good Fate protect thee from a Criticks power,
For If he comes, thou'rt gon in half an hour,
Stifl'd and blasted, 'tis their usual way,
To make that Night, which is as bright as Day.
For if they once but wring, and skrew their mouth,
Cock up their Hats, and set the point Du-South,
Armes all a kimbo, and with belly strut,
As if they had *Parnassus* in their gut:
These are the Symtomes of the murthering fall
Of my poor Infant, and his burial.
Say he should miss thee, and some ign'rant Asse
Should find thee out, as he along doth pass,
It were all one, he'd look into thy Tayle,
To see if thou wert Feminine or Male;

---

* During the quarrel between the army and parliament, Colonel
Pride, for whom this sarcasm was intended — acting under the direc-
tion of a council of officers and with the assistance of a regiment of
foot — excluded from the house of commons one hundred or more
members who favored the restoration of Charles as king. This has
since been known as " Pride's purge."

When he'd half starv'd thee, for to satisfie
His peeping Ign'rance, he'd then let thee lie;
And vow by's wit he ne're could understand,
The Heathen dresses of another Land:
Well, 'tis no matter, wherever such as he
Knows one grain, more than his simplicity.
Now, how the pulses of my Senses beat,
To think the rigid Fortune thou wilt meet;
Asses and captious Fools, not six in ten
Of thy Spectators will be real men,
To Umpire up the badness of the Cause,
And screen my weakness from the rav'nous Laws,
Of those that will undoubted sit to see
How they might blast this new-born Infancy:
If they should burn him, they'd conclude hereafter,
'Twere too good death for him to dye a Martyr;
And if they let him live, they think it will
Be but a means for to encourage ill,
And bring in time some strange *Antipod'ans*,
A thousand Leagues beyond *Philippians*,
To storm our Wits; therefore he must not rest,
But shall be hang'd, for all he has been prest:
Thus they conclude.— My Genius comforts give,
In Resurrection he will surely live.

To my Friend Mr. *George Alsop*, on his *Character*
of *MARY-LAND*.

WHo such odd nookes of Earths great mass describe,
    Prove their descent from old Columbus *tribe:*
Some Boding augur did his Name devise,
Thy Genius too cast in th' same mould and size ;
His Name predicted he would be a Rover,
And hidden places of this Orb discover ;
He made relation of that World in gross,
Thou the particulars retail'st to us :
By this first Peny of thy fancy we
Discover what thy greater Coines will be ;
This Embryo thus well polisht doth presage,
The manly Atchievements of its future age.
Auspicious winds blow gently on this spark,
Untill its flames discover what's yet dark ;
Mean while this short Abridgement we embrace,
Expecting that thy busie Soul will trace
Some Mines at last which may enrich the World,
And all that poverty may be in oblivion hurl'd.
Zoilus *is dumb, for thou the mark hast hit,*
By interlacing History with Wit :
Thou hast describ'd its superficial Treasure,
Anatomiz'd its bowels at thy leasure ;
That **MARY-LAND** *to thee may duty owe,*
Who to the World dost all her Glory shew :
Then thou shalt make the Prophesie fall true,
Who fill'st the World (like th' Sea) with knowledge new.
William Bogherst.

To my Friend Mr. *George Alsop*, on his *Character* of *MARY-LAND*.

*T*His *plain, yet pithy and concise Description*
   Of Mary-Lands *plentious and sedate condition,*
With other things herein by you set forth,
To shew its Rareness, and declare its Worth ;
Compos'd in such a time, when most men were
Smitten with Sickness, or surpriz'd with Fear,
Argues a Genius good, and Courage stout,
In bringing this Design so well about :
Such generous Freedom waited on thy brain,
The Work was done in midst of greatest pain ;
And matters flow'd so swiftly from thy source,
Nature design'd thee (sure) for such Discourse.
Go on then with thy Work so well begun,
Let it come forth, and boldly see the Sun ;
Then shall't be known to all, that from thy Youth
Thou heldst it Noble to maintain the Truth,
'Gainst all the Rabble-rout, that yelping stand,
To cast aspersions on thy MARY-LAND:
But this thy Work shall vindicate its Fame,
And as a Trophy memorize thy Name,
So if without a Tomb thou buried be,
This Book's a lasting Monument for thee.

                H. W., Master of Arts.

From my Study,
Jan. 10. 1665.

To my Friend Mr. *George Alsop,* on his *Character* of *MARY-LAND.*

COlumbus *with* Apollo *sure did set,*
When he did Court to propigate thy Wit,
Or else thy Genius with so small a Clew,
Could not have brought such Intricates in view ;
Discover'd hidden Earth so plain, that we
View more in this, then if we went to see,
MARY - LAND, *I with some thousands more,*
Could not imagine where she stood before ;
And hadst thou still been silent with thy Pen,
We had continu'd still the self-same men,
Ne're to have known the glory of that Soyle,
Whose plentious dwellings is four thousand mile.
The portly Susquehanock *in his naked dress,*
Had certain still been Pigmye, *or much less ;*
All had been dark (to us) and obscure yet,
Had not thy diligence discover'd it :
For this we owe thee Praises to the Skie,
But none but MARY - LAND *can gratifie.*

Will. Barber.*

---

* Our knowledge of those who wrote the preceding verses to our author is confined to that gathered from this book. Those written by Will. Barber were omitted in the Gowans reprint

A Land-Skip of the
Province of
MARY LAND
Or the
Lord Baltemore's
Plantation neere
Virginia
By Geo: Alsop Gent.

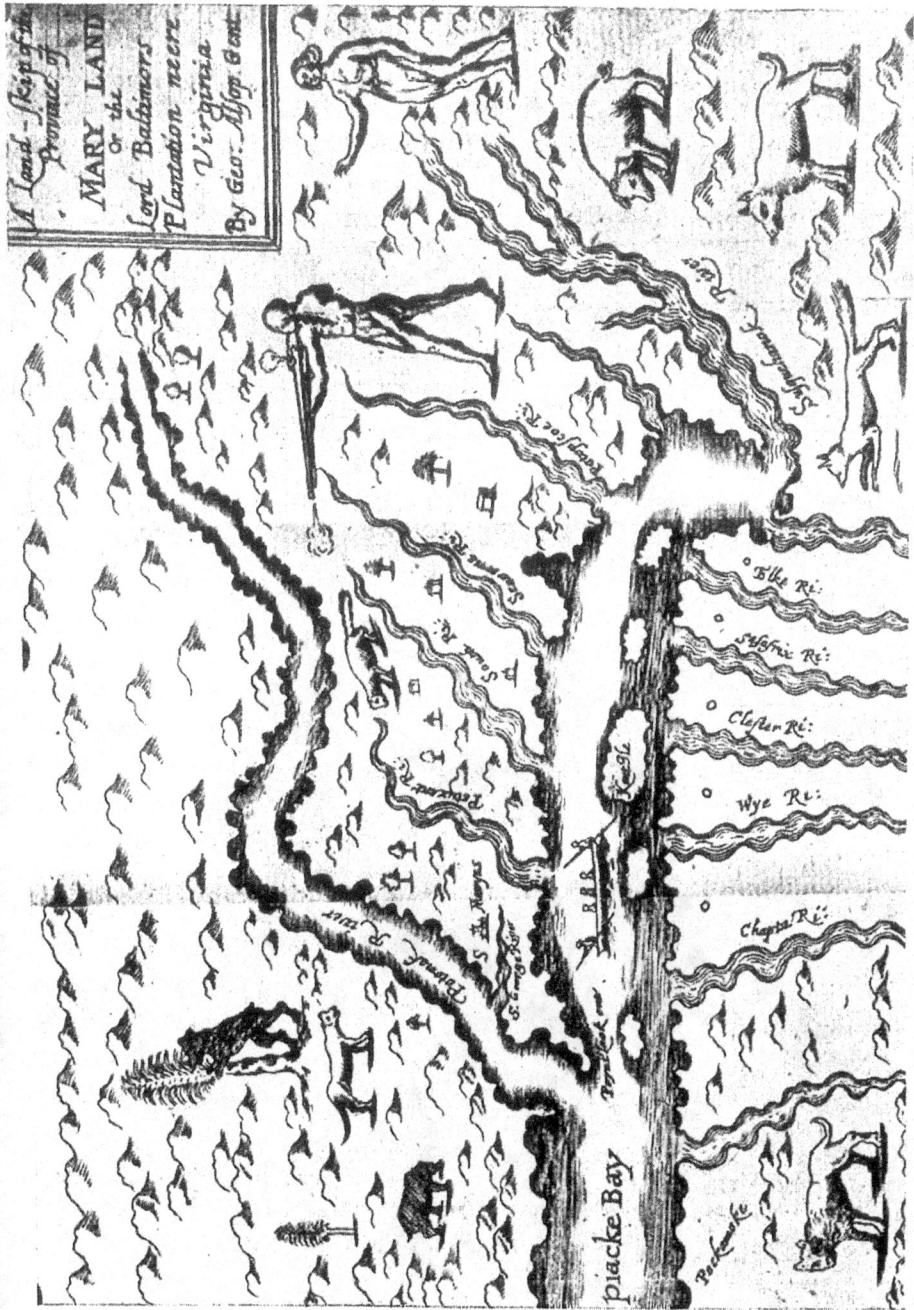

Susquehanok River

Elke Ri:

Sassafre Ri:

Chester Ri:

Wye Ri:

Choptanke Ri:

Kent Ile

Patapsco R.

Severn R.

South Ri:

Patuxent R.

Patapsco River

S. Maries River

S. Georges River

Chesopeacke Bay

Pocomocke

A

CHARACTER

MARY-LAND.

CHAP. I.

Of the situation and plenty of the Province of Mary-Land.

MARY-LAND is a Province situated upon the large extending bowels of *America*, under the Government of the Lord *Baltemore*, adjacent Northwardly upon the Confines of *New-England*, and neighbouring Southwardly upon *Virginia*, dwelling pleasantly upon the Bay of *Chœsapike*, between the Degrees of 36 and 38,* in

---

* In 1606 James I. formed two companies by a single charter. To one, the London Company, he granted the Atlantic coast of North America between latitude 34 and 38 degrees; to the other, the Plymouth Company, he granted that coast between latitude 41 and 45 degrees. The intervening space was to be common to both, but neither was to plant a settlement within one hundred miles of a previous settlement of the other. The grant to the London Company received the name of Virginia, and that to the Plymouth Company, of New England. The London Company surrendered its charter in the year 1624; and eight years later the coast from a point a trifle south of latitude 38 degrees northward to latitude 40 degrees was included in the grant of Maryland. But in 1681 William Penn received the grant of Pennsylvania and then arose that boundary dispute which resulted in the loss to Maryland, in 1685, of what is now the state of Delaware, and finally, in 1767, of a strip twenty miles wide along her entire northern border. Alsop should have said between the degrees 38 and 40 instead of 36 and 38.

the Zone temperate, and by Mathematical computation is eleven hundred and odd Leagues in Longitude from *England*, being within her own imbraces extraordinary pleasant and fertile. Pleasant, in respect of the multitude of Navigable Rivers and Creeks that conveniently and most profitably lodge within the armes of her green, spreading, and delightful Woods; whose natural womb (by her plenty) maintains and preserves the several diversities of Animals that rangingly inhabit her Woods; as she doth otherwise generously fructifie this piece of Earth with almost all sorts of Vegetables, as well Flowers with their varieties of colours and smells, as Herbes and Roots with their several effects and operative virtues, that offer their benefits daily to supply the want of the Inhabitant whene're their necessities shall *Sub-pœna* them to wait on their commands. So that he, who out of curiosity desires to see the Landskip of the Creation drawn to the life, or to read Natures universal Herbal without book, may with the Opticks of a discreet discerning, view *Mary-Land* drest in her green and fragrant Mantle of the Spring. Neither do I think there is any place under the Heavenly altitude, or that has footing or room upon the circular Globe of this world, that can parallel this fertile and pleasant piece of ground in its multiplicity, or rather Natures extravagancy of a superabounding plenty.* For so much doth this Country increase in a swelling Spring-tide of rich variety and diversities of all things, not only common provisions that supply the reaching stomach of man with a satisfactory plenty, but also extends with its liberality and free convenient benefits to each sensitive faculty, according to their several desiring Appetites. So that had Nature made it her business, on purpose to have found out a situation for the Soul of profitable Ingenuity, she could not have fitted herself better in the traverse of the whole Universe, nor in convenienter terms have told man, *Dwell here, live plentifully and be rich.*

The Trees, Plants, Fruits, Flowers, and Roots that grow here in *Mary-Land*, are the only Emblems or Hieroglyphicks of our Adamitical or Primitive situation, as well for their variety as odoriferous smells, together with their vertues, according to their several effects, kinds and properties, which still bear the Effigies of Innocency according to their original Grafts; which by their dumb vegetable Oratory, each hour speaks to the Inhabitant in silent acts, That they need not look for any other Terrestrial Paradice, to suspend or tyre their curiosity upon, while she is extant. For

---

* " Maryland is considered the most fertile portion of North America."— *Dankers and Sluyters* in *Memorials of the Long Island Historical Society*, vol. I., p. 194. " The mould is black, a foot deep."— *A Relation of Maryland* (1634), p. 22.

within her doth dwell so much of variety, so much
of natural plenty, that there is not any thing that
is or may be rare, but it inhabits within this plentious soyle: So that those parts of the Creation
that have borne the Bell away (for many ages)
for a vegetable plentiousness, must now in silence
strike and vayle all, and whisper softly in the
auditual parts of *Mary-Land*, that *None but she in
this dwells singular ;* and that as well for that she
doth exceed in those Fruits, Plants, Trees and
Roots, that dwell and grow in their several
Clymes or habitable parts of the Earth besides, as
the rareness and super-excellency of her own
glory, which she flourishly abounds in, by the
abundancy of reserved Rarities, such as the
remainder of the World (with all its speculative
art) never bore any occular testimony of as yet.
I shall forbear to particularize those several sorts
of vegetables that flourishingly grows here, by
reason of the vast tediousness that will attend
upon the description, which therefore makes them
much more fit for an Herbal, than a small Manu-
script or History.*

---

* Originally the eastern shore contained pine with some hard wood,
the central portion was covered with forests of hard woods, and the
northwest portion was covered with mixed forests of white pine,
hemlock, and hard wood. Although the most that was valuable for
timber has been cut, there yet remains some pine, hemlock, cedar,
oak, hickory, walnut, maple, ash, spruce, cypress, birch, chestnut,
poplar, and basswood.

" On the plains and in the open fields there is a great abundance
of grass; but the country is, for the most part, thickly wooded. There

As for the wilde Animals of this Country, which loosely inhabits the Woods in multitudes, it is impossible to give you an exact description of them all, considering the multiplicity as well as the diversity of so numerous an extent of Creatures: But such as has fallen within the compass or prospect of my knowledge, those you shall know of; *videlicet*, the Deer, because they are oftner seen, and more participated of by the Inhabitants of the Land, whose acquaintance by a customary familiarity becomes much more common than the rest of Beasts that inhabit the Woods by using themselves in Herds about the Christian Plantations. Their flesh, which in some places of this Province is the common provision the Inhabitants feed on, and which through the extreme glut and plenty of it, being daily killed by the *Indians*, and brought in to the *English*, as well as that which is killed by the Christian Inhabitant, that

are a great many hickory trees, and the oaks are so straight and tall, that beams, sixty feet long and two and one half feet wide, can be made of them. The cypress trees also grow to a height of eighty feet before they have branches, and three men with arms extended can barely reach around their trunks; and there are plenty of mulberry trees to feed silkworms. . . . There are alder, ash, and chestnut trees as large as those which grow in Spain, Italy, and France; and cedars equalling those which Libanus speaks of. . . . The woods moreover are passable, not filled with thorns or undergrowth, but arranged by nature for the production of animals, and for affording pleasure to man. . . . Peaches also are so abundant that an honorable and reliable man positively declared that he gave a hundred bushels to his pigs last year."— *Relatio Itineris*, pp. 49, 50, 52. See also *A Relation of Maryland* (1635), pp. 20, 22; and *Dankers and Sluyters*, pp. 193, 194, 200.

doth it more for recreation, than for the benefit they reap by it. I say, the flesh of Venison becomes (as to food) rather denyed, than any way esteemed or desired. And this I speak from an experimental knowledge; For when I was under a Command, and debarr'd of a four years ranging Liberty in the Province of *Mary-Land*, the Gentleman whom I served my conditional and prefixed time withall, had at one time in his house fourscore Venisons, besides plenty of other provisions to serve his Family nine months, they being but seven in number; so that before this Venison was brought to a period by eating, it so nauseated our appetites and stomachs, that plain bread was rather courted and desired than it.*

The Deer here neither in shape nor action differ from our Deer in *England* : The Park they traverse their ranging and unmeasured walks in, is bounded and impanell'd in with no other pales then the rough and billowed Ocean: They are also mighty numerous in the Woods, and are little or not at all affrighted at the face of a man, but (like the Does of *Whetstons* Park †) though their hydes are not altogether so gaudy to extract an

---

* " There are such numbers of swine and deer that they are rather an annoyance than an advantage."— *Relatio Itineris*, p. 51.

† It is doubtful if this place ever was well known as a park. In Alsop's day it must have been somewhat in the country. In the London of to-day there is a street by the name of Whetstone Park in Lincoln's Inn Fields at the back of Holborn.

admiration from the beholder, yet they will stand (all most) till they be scratcht.

As for the Wolves, Bears, and Panthers of this Country, they inhabit commonly in great multi-tudes up in the remotest parts of the Continent; yet at some certain time they come down near the Plantations, but do little hurt or injury worth noting,* and that which they do is of so degener-ate and low a nature, (as in reference to the fierceness and heroick vigour that dwell in the same kind of Beasts in other Countries), that they are hardly worth mentioning: For the highest of their designs and circumventing reaches is but cowardly and base, only to steal a poor Pigg, or kill a lost and half starved Calf. The Effigies of a man terrifies them dreadfully, for they no sooner espy him but their hearts are at their mouths, and the spurs upon their heels, they (having no more manners than Beasts) gallop away, and never bid them farewell that are behind them.

The Elke, the Cat of the Mountain,† the Rac-koon, the Fox, the Beaver, the Otter, the Possum, the Hare, the Squirril, the Monack,‡ the Musk-

---

* By an act of assembly, first passed in the year 1658, a bounty of one hundred pounds of tobacco was offered for every wolf that should be killed.

† Catamount was the name usually given by the colonists to this animal *(Felis concolor)*. In our day it is more often called cougar, puma, or American lion.

‡ Undoubtedly this was intended to designate that animal which is now commonly called the woodchuck *(Arctomys monax)*.

Rat, and several others (whom I'le omit for brevity sake) inhabit here in *Mary-Land* in several droves and troops, ranging the Woods at their pleasure.*

The meat of most of these Creatures is good for eating, yet of no value nor esteem here, by reason of the great plenty of other provisions, and are only kill'd by the *Indians* of the Country for their Hydes and Furrs, which become very profitable to those that have the right way of traffiquing for them, as well as it redounds to the *Indians* that take the pains to catch them, and to flay and dress their several Hydes, selling and disposing them for such Commodities as their Heathenish fancy delights in.

As for those Beasts that were carried over at the first seating of the Country, to stock and increase the situation, as Cows, Horses, Sheep and Hogs,† they are generally tame, and use near home, especially the Cows, Sheep and Horses. The Hogs, whose increase is innumerable in the Woods, do disfrequent home more than the rest of Creatures that are look'd upon as tame, yet with little trouble and pains they are slain and

---

* " In the upper parts of the country there are buffaloes, elks, lions, bears, wolves, and deer there are in great store in all places that are not too much frequented, as also beavers, foxes, otters, and many other sorts of beasts."— *A Relation of Maryland* (1635), pp. 22, 23.

† Cows, swine, and poultry came chiefly from Virginia, but horses and sheep could not be obtained there. Wild horses and wild swine were in abundance, but of sheep there were few during the entire colonial era; and the census of 1900 gives for the state only 1193 sheep, but 38,525 horses, 36,616 swine, and 12,950 cattle.

made provision of. Now they that will with a right Historical Survey, view the Woods of *Mary-Land* in this particular, as in reference to Swine, must upon necessity judge this Land lineally descended from the *Gadarean* Territories.*

Mary-Land (I must confess) cannot boast of her plenty of Sheep here, as other Countries; not but that they will thrive and increase here, as well as in any place of the World besides, but few desire them, because they commonly draw down the Wolves among the Plantations, as well by the sweetness of their flesh, as by the humility of their nature, in not making a defensive resistance against the rough dealing of a ravenous Enemy. They who for curiosity will keep Sheep, may expect that after the Wolves have breathed them-selves all day in the Woods to sharpen their stomachs, they will come without fail and sup with them at night, though many times they surfeit themselves with the sawce that's dish'd out of the muzzle of a Gun, and so in the midst of their banquet (poor Animals) they often sleep with their Ancestors.

Fowls of all sorts and varieties dwell at their several times and seasons here in *Mary-Land:* The Turkey, the Woodcock, the Pheasant, the Partrich, the Pigeon, and others, especially the Turkey, whom I have seen in whole hundreds in

*See St. Luke, viii., 26-33.

flights in the Woods of *Mary-Land*, being an extra-ordinary fat Fowl, whose flesh is very pleasant and sweet.* These Fowls that I have named are intayled from generation to generation to the Woods. The Swans, the Geese and Ducks (with other Water-Fowl) derogate in this point of setled residence; for they arrive in millionous multitudes in *Mary-Land* about the middle of *September*, and take their winged farewell about the midst of *March:* † But while they do remain, and beleagure the borders of the shoar with their winged Dra-goons, several of them are summoned by a Writ of *Fieri facias*, to answer their presumptuous con-tempt upon a Spit.

---

* '' There are great quantities of wild turkeys, which are twice as large as our tame and domestic ones."— *Relatio Itineris*, p. 52. '' Wild turkeys in great abundance, whereof many weigh fifty pounds and upward."— *A Relation of Maryland* (1635), p. 23.

† '' I have nowhere seen so many ducks together as were in the creek in front of this house. The water was so black with them that it seemed when you looked up from the land below upon the water, as if it were a mass of filth or turf, and when they flew up there was a rushing and vibration of the air like a great storm coming through the trees, and even like the rumbling of distant thunder, while the sky over the whole creek was filled with them like a cloud. . . . I must not forget to mention the great number of wild geese we saw here on the river. They rose in flocks not of ten or twelve, or twenty or thirty, but continually, wherever we pushed our way; and as they made room for us, there was such an incessant clattering made with their wings on the water where they rose, and such a noise of those flying higher up, that it was as if we were all the time surrounded by a whirlwind or a storm. This proceeded not only from geese, but from ducks and other water fowl; and it is not peculiar to this place alone, but it occurred on all the creeks and rivers we crossed, though they were most numerous in the morning and evening when they are most easily shot."— *Dankers and Sluyters*, pp. 204, 208.

As for Fish, which dwell in the watry tene-
ments of the deep, and by a providential greatness
of power, is kept for the relief of several Countries in the world (which would else sink under
the rigid enemy of want), here in *Mary-Land* is a
large sufficiency, and plenty of almost all sorts of
Fishes, which live and inhabit within her several
Rivers and Creeks, far beyond the apprehending
or crediting of those that never saw the same,
which with very much ease is catched, to the great
refreshment of the Inhabitants of the Province.*

All sorts of Grain, as Wheat, Rye, Barley,
Oates, Pease, besides several others that have
their original and birth from the fertile womb of
this Land (and no where else), they all grow,
increase, and thrive here in *Mary-Land*, without
the chargable and laborious manuring of the
Land with Dung; increasing in such a measure
and plenty, by the natural richness of the Earth,
with the common, beneficial and convenient
showers of rain that usually wait upon the several
Fields of Grain (by a natural instinct), so that
Famine (the dreadful Ghost of penury and want)

---

* " The sea, the bays of Chesapeake and Delaware, and generally
all the rivers, do abound with fish of several sorts; for many of them
we have no English names: there are whales, sturgeons, very large
and good and in great abundance; grampuses, porpuses, mullets,
trout, mackerel, perch, crabs, oysters, cockles, and mussels. But
above all these, the fish that have no English names are the best,
except sturgeons."— *A Relation of Maryland* (1635), p. 23. See
also *Relatio Itineris*, pp. 48, 49, 51; and *Dankers and Sluyters*,
p. 195.

is never known with his pale visage to haunt the
Dominions of *Mary-Land.**

> *Could'st thou (O Earth) live thus obscure, and now*
> *Within an Age, shew forth thy plentious brow*
> *Of rich variety, gilded with fruitful Fame,*
> *That (Trumpet-like) doth Heraldize thy Name,*
> *And tells the World there is a Land now found,*
> *That all Earth's Globe can't parallel its Ground?*
> *Dwell, and be prosperous, and with thy plenty feed*
> *The craving Carkesses of those Souls that need.*

CHAP. II.

Of the Government and Natural disposition of the People.

MARY-LAND, not from the remoteness of
her situation, but from the regularity of
her well ordered Government, may (without sin,
I think) be called *Singular:* And though she is
not supported with such large Revenues as some
of her Neighbours are, yet such is her wisdom in

---

* As a matter of fact there was but little English grain grown in the
province before about the year 1735. From the beginning, an act of
assembly required that for every one working in tobacco at least two
acres of corn should be planted under penalty of two hundred pounds
of tobacco for each acre in default. An act for the encouragement
of the sowing of English grain, first passed in the year 1662, had
little effect; and corn continued to be the main cereal for master,
servant, and beast. See *A Relation of Maryland* (1635), pp. 27, 28;
Relatio Itineris, p. 52; *Dankers and Sluyters*, pp. 191, 197, 211,
212, 217; and Mereness's *Maryland as a Proprietary Province*, pp.
120–125.

a reserved silence, and not in pomp, to shew her well-conditioned Estate, in relieving at a distance the proud poverty of those that wont be seen they want, as well as those which by undeniable necessities are drove upon the Rocks of pinching wants: Yet such a loathsome creature is a common and folding-handed Beggar, that upon the penalty of almost a perpetual working in Imprisonment, they are not to appear, nor lurk near our vigilant and laborious dwellings. The Country hath received a general spleen and antipathy against the very name and nature of it; and though there were no Law provided (as there is) to suppress it, I am certainly confident, there is none within the Province that would lower themselves so much below the dignity of men to beg, as long as limbs and life keep house together; so much is a vigilant industrious care esteem'd.

He that desires to see the real Platform of a quiet and sober Government extant, Superiority with a meek and yet commanding power sitting at the Helme, steering the actions of State quietly, through the multitude and diversity of Opinionous waves that diversely meet, let him look on *Mary-Land* with eyes admiring, and he'le then judge her, *The Miracle of this Age.*

Here the *Roman Catholick*, and the *Protestant Episcopal*, (whom the world would perswade have proclaimed open Wars irrevocably against each other) contrarywise concur in an unanimous parallel of friendship, and inseparable love intayled unto one another: * All Inquisitions, Martyrdom, and Banishments are not so much as named, but unexpressably abhorr'd by each other.

The several Opinions and Sects that lodge within this Government, meet not together in mutinous contempts to disquiet the power that bears Rule, but with a reverend quietness obeys the legal commands of Authority.† Here's never seen Five Monarchies in a Zealous Rebellion, opposing the Rights and Liberties of a true setled Government, or Monarchical Authority: ‡ Nor did I ever see (here in *Mary-Land*) any of those

---

* There was in general no such good feeling as this between Catholics and Protestants. See Mereness's *Maryland as a Proprietary Province*, p. 435 *et seq.*

† In July, 1659, because of the insubordination of a few Quakers, who had recently come into the province, Governor Fendall and his council passed an order directing that such Quakers as returned after having been once banished should be whipped from constable to constable until they were again out of the province; but this order remained in force for little more than one year and it is not certain that there was a single instance of its execution.

‡ The fifth monarchy men were a religious sect that appeared in England during the period of the Commonwealth. They believed that the time had come for the establishment of the " fifth monarchy," the one to succeed the Assyrian, the Persian, the Grecian, and the Roman, and over which Christ with his saints should reign a thousand years. After the Restoration, in January, 1661, fifty of them, under the leadership of a wine-cooper named Venner, attempted to take possession of London in the name of " King Jesus." In this attempt the most of them were either killed or taken prisoners, and the same month Venner and ten others were executed for high treason.

dancing Adamitical Sisters, that plead a primitive
Innocency for their base obscenity, and naked
deportment; but I conceive if some of them were
there at some certain time of the year, between the
Months of *January* and *February*, when the winds
blow from the North-West quarter of the world,
that it would both cool, and (I believe) convert
the hottest of these Zealots from their burning
and fiercest Concupiscence.

The Government of this Province doth continually, by all lawful means, strive to purge her
Dominions from such base corroding humors,
that would predominate upon the least smile of
Liberty, did not the Laws check and bridle in
those unwarranted and tumultuous Opinions.
And truly, where a Kingdom, State or Government, keeps or cuts down the weeds of destructive
Opinions, there must certainly be a blessed Har-
mony of quietness. And I really believe this
Land or Government of *Mary-Land* may boast,
that she enjoys as much quietness from the dis-
turbance of Rebellious Opinions, as most States or
Kingdoms do in the world: For here every man
lives quietly, and follows his labour and imployment desiredly; and by the protection of the
Laws, they are supported from those molestious
troubles that ever attend upon the Commons
of other States and Kingdoms, as well as from
the Aquafortial operation of great and eating

Taxes.* Here's nothing to be levyed out of the Granaries of Corn; but contrarywise, by a Law every Domestick Governor of a Family is enjoyned to make or cause to be made so much Corn by a just limitation, as shall be sufficient for him and his Family: So that by this wise and *Janus*-like providence, the thin-jawed Skeliton with his starv'd Carkess is never seen walking the Woods of *Mary-Land* to affrighten Children.

Once every year within this Province is an Assembly called, and out of every respective County (by the consent of the people) there is chosen a number of men, and to them is deliver'd up the Grievances of the Country; and they maturely debate the matters, and according to their Consciences make Laws for the general good of the people; and where any former Law that was made, seems and is prejudicial to the good or

---

* An act of assembly, in force subsequent to the year 1650, forbade the levying of any subsidy, aid, customs, tax, or imposition upon the freemen of Maryland before the consent of their representatives in assembly had been first obtained. The year in which our author wrote there was imposed a poll-tax of twenty-five pounds of tobacco, a port duty of one-half pound of powder and three pounds of shot (or their equivalent) per ton, and each county, by a poll-tax, paid for the food and lodging of its delegates during a session of assembly, as well as the ferry expenses incurred. For a few years prior to this the delegates had been paid for each day's service in assembly and the expense of a few small expeditions against the Indians had been incurred. Otherwise the taxes had hitherto been even less. The officers of the government were, however, supported by fees, by the sale of licenses, and by fines and forfeitures more than by taxes and duties. See Mereness's *Maryland as a Proprietary Province*, pp. 171–174, 181, 182, 249–251, 319, *et seq.*

quietness of the Land, it is repeal'd. These men that determine on these matters for the Republique, are called Burgesses, and they commonly sit in Junto about six weeks, being for the most part good ordinary Householders of the several Counties, which do more by a plain and honest Conscience, than by artificial Syllogisms drest up in gilded Orations.*

Here Suits and Tryals in Law seldome hold dispute two Terms or Courts, but according as the Equity of the Cause appears is brought to a period. The *Temples* and *Grays-Inne* are clear out of fashion here: *Marriot*† would sooner get a

---

* Previous to the year 1650 the freemen met in assembly in person, or were represented there either by proxies privately chosen or by delegates publicly elected; but in that and subsequent years they were represented in that body by delegates only. Until 1654 representation was by hundreds, but from that time it was by counties — four from each except for a short interval. In 1649 or 1650 the assembly which had hitherto sat as one house was divided into two — the council, at first with the governor but later without him, constituting the upper house, and the people's delegates the lower. For a time the lord proprietor attempted to reserve to himself or to the governor in council the sole right of initiating legislation, but this he surrendered in 1638. From 1666 to 1669, from 1671 to 1674, and from 1681 to 1684 there was no session of the assembly, but with these exceptions there was scarcely a year of proprietary government in which that body did not meet at least once; and with but two exceptions, when the interval was about five years, there never was a time under that government in which there was not an election of delegates after an interval of about three years or less.

† "Marriott, John (d. 1653), 'the great eater,' familiarly known as Ben Marriott, is said to have been a respectable lawyer, who entered Gray's Inn during the reign of James I., and at the time of his death, in 1653, was the patriarch of the society. . . . He became notorious in the year previous to his death owing to the circulation

paunch-devouring meal for nothing, then for his invading Counsil. Here if the Lawyer had nothing else to maintain him but his bawling, he might button up his Chops, and burn his Buckrom Bag, or else hang it upon a pin untill its Antiquity had eaten it up with durt and dust: Then with a Spade, like his Grandsire *Adam*, turn up the face of the Creation, purchasing his bread by the sweat of his brows, that before was got by the motionated Water-works of his jaws.* So contrary to the Genius of the people, if not to the quiet Government of the Province, that the turbulent Spirit of continued and vexatious Law, with all its querks and evasions, is openly and most eagerly opposed, that might make matters either dubious, tedious, or troublesom.† All other matters that would be ranging in contrary and improper Spheres, (in short) are here by the Power moderated, lower'd and subdued. All villanous Outrages that are committed in other States, are not so much as known here: A man may walk in the open Woods as secure from being externally dissected, as in his own house or dwelling. So hateful is a Robber, that if but once imagin'd to

---

of a malicious and licentious pasquinade, entitled, ' The Great Eater of Graye's Inn, or the Life of Mr. Marriott, the Cormorant.' " — *Dictionary of National Biography*.

*Lawyers were, indeed, scarce in Maryland during the seventeenth century, but were somewhat numerous and influential in the eighteenth.

† Contrast this with Cook's *The Sot-Weed Factor*, pp. 15, 16.

be so, he's kept at a distance, and shun'd as the Pestilential noysomness.*

It is generally and very remarkably observed, That those whose Lives and Conversations have had no other gloss nor glory stampt on them in their own Country, but the stigmatization of base-ness, were here (by the common civilities and deportments of the Inhabitants of this Province) brought to detest and loath their former actions. Here the Constable hath no need of a train of Holberteers, that carry more Armour about them, then heart to guard him: Nor is he ever troubled to leave his Feathered Nest to some friendly suc-cessor, while he is placing of his Lanthern-horn Guard at the end of some suspicious Street, to catch some Night-walker, or Batchelor of Leach-ery, that has taken his Degree three story high in a Bawdy-house. Here's no *Newgates* for pilfering Felons, nor *Ludgates* for Debtors, nor any *Bride-wels* † to lash the soul of Concupiscence into a chast Repentance. For as there is none of these Prisons in *Mary-Land*,‡ so the merits of the Coun-

---

* Maryland seems to have been quite free from robberies until the middle of the eighteenth century, when, for a time, some convict servants, sent over from England, renewed their former practice.

† Newgate, Ludgate, and Bridewell are well known London prisons.

‡ It was in the year 1662 that the assembly made its first appropria-tion for a prison at St. Marys, and only a few years later that body directed the justices of each county to provide their county with a prison, a pillory, stocks, a whipping-post, and a burning-iron.

try deserves none, but if any be foully vitious, he is so reserv'd in it, that he seldom or never becomes popular. Common Alehouses, (whose dwellings are the only Receptacles of debauchery and baseness, and those Schools that trains up Youth, as well as Age, to ruine) in this Province there are none; * neither hath Youth his swing or range in such a profuse and unbridled liberty as in other Countries; for from an antient Custom at the primitive seating of the place, the Son works as well as the Servant (an excellent cure for untam'd Youth), so that before they eat their bread, they are commonly taught how to earn it; which makes them by that time Age speaks them capable of receiving that which their Parents indulgency is ready to give them, and which partly is by their own laborious industry purchased, they manage it with such a serious, grave and watching care, as if they had been Masters of Families, trained up in that domestick and governing power from their Cradles. These Christian Natives of the Land, especially those of

---

* Only thirteen years later Dankers and Sluyters wrote of these same people in their journal: "When the ships arrive with goods, and especially with liquors, such as wine and brandy, they attract everybody, that is, masters, to them, who then indulge so abominably together, that they keep nothing for the rest of the year, yea, do not go away as long as there is any left, or bring any thing home with them which might be useful to them in their subsequent necessities. . . . They squander so much in this way, that they keep no tobacco to buy a shoe or a stocking for their children which sometimes causes great misery."

the Masculine Sex, are generally conveniently confident, reservedly subtle, quick in apprehending, but slow in resolving; and where they spy profit sailing towards them with the wings of a prosperous gale, there they become much familiar. The Women differ something in this point, though not much: They are extreme bashful at the first view, but after a continuance of time hath brought them acquainted, there they become discreetly familiar, and are much more talkative then men. All Complemental Courtships, drest up in critical Rarities, are meer strangers to them, plain wit comes nearest their Genius; so that he that intends to Court a *Mary-Land* Girle, must have something more than the Tautologies of a long-winded speech to carry on his design, or else he may (for ought I know) fall under the contempt of her frown, and his own windy Oration.

One great part of the Inhabitants of this Province are desiredly Zealous, great pretenders to Holiness; and where any thing appears that carries on the Frontispiece of its Effigies the stamp of Religion, though fundamentally never so imperfect, they are suddenly taken with it, and out of an eager desire to any thing that's new, not weighing the sure matter in the Ballance of Reason, are very apt to be catcht.* *Quakerism* is the only Opinion that bears the Bell away: The

* This is our author's habitual way of talking about the Puritans.

Anabaptists have little to say here, as well as in other places, since the Ghost of *John of Leyden* haunts their Conventicles. The *Adamite, Ranter,* and *Fift-Monarchy men, Mary-Land* cannot, nay will not digest within her liberal stomach such corroding morsels: So that this Province is an utter Enemy to blasphemous and zealous Imprecations, drain'd from the Lymbeck of hellish and damnable Spirits, as well as profuse prophaness, that issues from the prodigality of none but cract-brain Sots.

'Tis said the Gods lower down that Chain above,
That tyes both Prince and Subject up in Love;
And if this Fiction of the Gods be true,
Few, **Mary-Land,** *in this can boast but you:*
Live ever blest, and let those Clouds that do
Eclipse most States, be alwayes Lights to you;
And dwelling so, you may for ever be
The only Emblem of Tranquility.

CHAP. III.

The necessariness of Servitude proved, with the common usage of Servants in Mary-Land, *together with their Priviledges.*

AS there can be no Monarchy without the Supremacy of a King and Crown, nor no King without Subjects, nor any Parents without it be by the fruitful off-spring of Children; neither

can there be any Masters, unless it be by the
inferior Servitude of those that dwell under them,
by a commanding enjoynment: And since it is
ordained from the original and superabounding
wisdom of all things, That there should be Degrees
and Diversities amongst the Sons of men, in
acknowledging of a Superiority from Inferiors to
Superiors; the Servant with a reverent and befit-
ting Obedience is as liable to this duty in a meas-
urable performance to him whom he serves, as the
loyalest of Subjects to his Prince. Then since it
is a common and ordained Fate, that there must
be Servants as well as Masters, and that good
Servitudes are those Colledges of Sobriety that
checks in the giddy and wild-headed youth from
his profuse and uneven course of life, by a limited
constrainment, as well as it otherwise agrees with
the moderate and discreet Servant: Why should
there be such an exclusive Obstacle in the minds
and unreasonable dispositions of many people,
against the limited time of convenient and necessary Servitude, when it is a thing so requisite,
that the best of Kingdoms would be unhing'd from
their quiet and well setled Government without
it. Which levelling doctrine we here of *England*
in this latter age (whose womb was truss'd out
with nothing but confused Rebellion) have too
much experienced, and was daily rung into the
ears of the tumultuous Vulgar by the Bell-weather

Sectaries of the Times: But (blessed be God) those Clouds are blown over, and the Government of the Kingdom coucht under a more stable form.

There is no truer Emblem of Confusion either in Monarchy or Domestick Governments, then when either the Subject, or the Servant, strives for the upper hand of his Prince, or Master, and to be equal with him, from whom he receives his present subsistance: Why then, if Servitude be so necessary that no place can be governed in order, nor people live without it, this may serve to tell those which prick up their ears and bray against it, That they are none but Asses, and deserve the Bridle of a strict commanding power to reine them in: For I'me certainly confident, that there are several Thousands in most Kingdoms of Christendom, that could not at all live and subsist, unless they had served some prefixed time, to learn either some Trade, Art, or Science, and by either of them to extract their present livelihood.

Then methinks this may stop the mouths of those that will undiscreetly compassionate them that dwell under necessary Servitudes; for let but Parents of an indifferent capacity in Estates, when their Childrens age by computation speak them seventeen or eighteen years old, turn them loose to the wide world, without a seven years working Apprenticeship (being just brought up to the bare formality of a little reading and writing) and you shall immediately see how weak and shiftless they'le be towards the maintaining and supporting of themselves; and (without either stealing or begging) their bodies like a Sentinel must continually wait to see when their Souls will be frighted away by the pale Ghost of a starving want.

Then let such, where Providence hath ordained to live as Servants, either in *England* or beyond Sea, endure the prefixed yoak of their limited time with patience, and then in a small computa- tion of years, by an industrious endeavour, they may become Masters and Mistresses of Families themselves. And let this be spoke to the deserved praise of *Mary-Land*, That the four years I served there were not to me so slavish, as a two years Servitude of a Handicraft Apprenticeship was here in *London ; Volenti enim nil difficile:* Not that I write this to seduce or delude any, or to draw them from their native soyle, but out of a love to my Countrymen, whom in the general I wish well to, and that the lowest of them may live in such a capacity of Estate, as that the bare interest of their Livelihoods might not altogether depend upon persons of the greatest extendments.

Now those whose abilities here in *England* are capable of maintaining themselves in any reason- able and handsom manner, they had best so to

remain, lest the roughness of the Ocean, together
with the staring visages of the wilde Animals,
which they may see after their arrival into the
Country, may alter the natural dispositions of
their bodies, that the stay'd and solid part that
kept its motion by Doctor *Trigs* purgationary
operation, may run beyond the byas of the wheel
in a violent and laxative confusion.

Now contrarywise, they who are low, and make
bare shifts to buoy themselves up above the shabby
center of beggarly and incident casualties, I
heartily could wish the removal of some of them
into *Mary-Land*, which would make much better
for them that stay'd behind, as well as it would
advantage those that went.

They whose abilities cannot extend to purchase
their own transportation over into *Mary-Land*, (and
surely he that cannot command so small a sum for
so great a matter, his life must needs be mighty low
and dejected)* I say they may for the debarment
of a four years sordid liberty, go over into this
Province and there live plentiously well. And
what's a four years Servitude to advantage a man
all the remainder of his dayes, making his prede-
cessors happy in his sufficient abilities, which he
attained to partly by the restrainment of so small
a time?

---

* The amount required for paying passage at this time was about
six pounds sterling.

Now those that commit themselves unto the care of the Merchant to carry them over, they need not trouble themselves with any inquisitive search touching their Voyage; for there is such an honest care and provision made for them all the time they remain aboard the Ship, and are sailing over, that they want for nothing that is necessary and convenient.

The Merchant commonly before they go aboard the Ship, or set themselves in any forwardness for their Voyage, has Conditions of Agreements drawn between him and those that by a voluntary consent become his Servants, to serve him, his Heirs or Assigns, according as they in their primitive acquaintance have made their bargain, some two, some three, some four years;* and whatever the Master or Servant tyes himself up to here in *England* by Condition, the Laws of the Province will force a performance of when they come there: Yet here is this Priviledge in it when they arrive, If they dwell not with the Merchant they made their first agreement withall, they may choose whom they will serve their prefixed time with; and after their curiosity has pitcht on one whom they think fit for their turn, and that they may live well withall, the Merchant makes an Assignment of the Indenture over to him whom

---

* This was the indenture, and those who came subject to one were called indentured, or indented, servants.

they of their free will have chosen to be their
Master,* in the same nature as we here in *England* (and no otherwise) turn over Covenant Servants or Apprentices from one Master to another.
Then let those whose chaps are always breathing
forth those filthy dregs of abusive exclamations,
which are Lymbeckt from their sottish and preposterous brains, against this Country of *Mary-Land*,
saying, That those which are transported over
thither, are sold in open Market for Slaves, and
draw in Carts like Horses; which is so damnable
an untruth, that if they should search to the very
Center of Hell, and enquire for a Lye of the most
antient and damned stamp, I confidently believe
they could not find one to parallel this: For
know, That the Servants here in *Mary-Land* of all
Colonies, distant or remote Plantations, have the
least cause to complain, either for strictness of
Servitude, want of Provisions, or need of Apparel: † Five dayes and a half in the Summer
weeks is the alotted time that they work in; and
for two months, when the Sun predominates in
the highest pitch of his heat, they claim an

---

* Servants who enjoyed the privilege of choosing their own master
upon their arrival in the province were called free-willers. In our
day these as well as those then called indented servants are commonly spoken of as redemptioners.

† We may readily believe that Alsop is here speaking too exclusively from his own experience to give a true picture of the general
treatment of servants in Maryland at this time. See *Dankers and
Sluyters*, pp. 191, 216; Eddis's *Letters from America*, pp. 63–89;
and Mereness's *Maryland as a Proprietary Province*, pp. 134–136.

antient and customary Priviledge, to repose themselves three hours in the day within the house,
and this is undeniably granted to them that work
in the Fields.

In the Winter time, which lasteth three months
(*viz.*) *December*, *January*, and *February*, they do
little or no work or imployment, save cutting of
wood to make good fires to sit by, unless their
Ingenuity will prompt them to hunt the Deer, or
Bear, or recreate themselves in Fowling, to
slaughter the Swans, Geese, and Turkeys (which
this Country affords in a most plentiful manner:)
For every Servant has a Gun, Powder and Shot
allowed him, to sport him withall on all Holidayes
and leasurable times, if he be capable of using it,
or be willing to learn.

Now those Servants which come over into this
Province, being Artificers, they never (during
their Servitude) work in the Fields, or do any
other imployment save that which their Handicraft and Mechanick endeavours are capable of
putting them upon, and are esteem'd as well by
their Masters, as those that imploy them, above
measure. He that's a Tradesman here in *Mary-
Land* (though a Servant), lives as well as most
common Handicrafts do in *London*,* though they
may want something of that Liberty which Free-

* Here, also, our author is perhaps speaking from experience more
than from observation.

men have, to go and come at their pleasure; yet if it were rightly understood and considered, what most of the Liberties of the several poor Tradesmen are taken up about, and what a care and trouble attends that thing they call Liberty, which according to the common translation is but Idleness, and (if weighed in the Ballance of a just Reason) will be found to be much heavier and cloggy then the four years restrainment of a *Mary-Land* Servitude. He that lives in the nature of a Servant in this Province, must serve but four years by the Custom of the Country; and when the expiration of his time speaks him a Freeman, there's a Law in the Province, that enjoyns his Master whom he hath served to give him Fifty Acres of Land, Corn to serve him a whole year, three Sutes of Apparel, with things necessary to them, and Tools to work withall; so that they are no sooner free, but they are ready to set up for themselves, and when once entred, they live passingly well.

The Women that go over into this Province as Servants, have the best luck here as in any place of the world besides; for they are no sooner on shoar, but they are courted into a Copulative Matrimony, which some of them (for aught I know) had they not come to such a Market with their Virginity, might have kept it by them untill it had been mouldy, unless they had let it out by a yearly rent to some of the Inhabitants of *Lewknors-lane*,* or made a Deed of Gift of it to Mother *Coney*, having only a poor stipend out of it, untill the Gallows or Hospital called them away. Men have not altogether so good luck as Women in this kind, or natural preferment, without they be good Rhetoricians, and well vers'd in the Art of perswasion, then (probably) they may ryvet themselves in the time of their Servitude into the private and reserved favour of their Mistress, if Age speak their Master deficient.

In short, touching the Servants of this Province, they live well in the time of their Service, and by their restrainment in that time, they are made capable of living much better when they come to be free; which in several other parts of the world I have observed, That after some servants have brought their indented and limited time to a just and legal period by Servitude, they have been much more incapable of supporting themselves from sinking into the Gulf of a slavish, poor, fettered, and intangled life, then all the fastness of their prefixed time did involve them in before.

Now the main and principal Reason of those incident casualties, that wait continually upon the residencies of most poor Artificers, is (I gather) from the multiplicity or innumerableness of those

---

* This was one of the disreputable places in the parish of St. Giles, London.

several Companies of Tradesmen, that dwell so closely and stiflingly together in one and the same place, that like the chafing Gum in Watered-Tabby, they eat into the folds of one anothers Estates. And this might easily be remedied, would but some of them remove and disperse distantly where want and necessity calls for them; their dwellings (I am confident) would be much larger, and their conditions much better, as well in reference to their Estates, as to the satisfactoriness of their minds, having a continual imployment, and from that imployment a continual benefit, without either begging, seducing, or flattering for it, encroaching that one month from one of the same profession, that they are heaved out themselves the next. For I have observed on the other side of *Mary-Land*, that the whole course of most Mechanical endeavours, is to catch, snatch, and undervalue one another, to get a little work, or a Customer; which when they have attained by their lowbuilt and sneaking circumventings, it stands upon so flashy, mutable, and transitory a foundation, that the best of his hopes is commonly extinguisht before the poor undervalued Tradesman is warm in the enjoyment of his Customer.

Then did not a cloud of low and base Cowardize eclipse the Spirits of these men, these things might easily be diverted; but they had as live

take a Bear by the tooth, as think of leaving their
own Country, though they live among their own
National people, and are governed by the same
Laws they have here, yet all this wont do with
them; and all the Reason they can render to the
contrary is, There's a great Sea betwixt them and
Mary-Land, and in that Sea there are Fishes, and
not only Fishes but great Fishes, and then should
a Ship meet with such an inconsiderable encounter
as a Whale, one blow with his tayle, and then
Lord have Mercy upon us: Yet meet with these
men in their common Exchange, which is one
story high in the bottom of a Celler, disputing
over a Black-pot, it would be monstrously dreadful here to insert the particulars, one swearing
that he was the first that scaled the Walls of
Dundee, when the Bullets flew about their ears as
thick as Hail-stones usually fall from the Sky;
which if it were but rightly examined, the most
dangerous Engagement that ever he was in, was
but at one of the flashy battels at *Finsbury,* where
commonly there's more Custard greedily devoured,
then men prejudiced by the rigour of the War.
Others of this Company relating their several
dreadful exploits, and when they are just entring
into the particulars, let but one step in and inter-
rupt their discourse, by telling them of a Sea
Voyage, and the violency of storms that attends
it, and that there are no back-doors to run out

at, which they call, *a handsom Retreat and Charge again;* the apprehensive danger of this is so powerful and penetrating on them, that a damp sweat immediately involves their Microcosm, so that *Margery* the old Matron of the Celler, is fain to run for a half-peny-worth of *Angelica* to rub their nostrils; and though the Port-hole of their bodies has been stopt from a convenient Evacuation some several months, they'le need no other Suppository to open the Orifice of their Esculent faculties then this Relation, as their Drawers or Breeches can more at large demonstrate to the inquisitive search of the curious.

Now I know that some will be apt to judge, that I have written this last part out of derision to some of my poor Mechanick Country-men: Truly I must needs tell those to their face that think so of me, that they prejudice me extremely, by censuring me as guilty of any such crime: What I have written is only to display the sordidness of their dispositions, who rather than they will remove to another Country to live plentiously well, and give their Neighbors more Elbow-room and space to breath in, they will croud and throng upon one another, with the pressure of a beggarly and unnecessary weight.

That which I have to say more in this business, is a hearty and desirous wish, that the several poor Tradesmen here in *London* that I know, and have borne an occular testimony of their want, might live so free from care as I did when I dwelt in the bonds of a four years Servitude in *Mary-Land.*

Be just (Domestick Monarchs) unto them
That dwell as Household Subjects to each Realm;
Let not your Power make you be too severe,
Where there's small faults reign in your sharp Career:
So that the Worlds base yelping Crew
May'nt bark what I have wrote is writ untrue,
So use your Servants, if there come no more,
They may serve Eight, instead of serving Four.

CHAP. IV.

Upon Trafique, and what Merchandizing Commodities this Province affords, also how Tobacco is planted and made fit for Commerce.

TRafique, Commerce, and Trade, are those great wheeles that by their circular and continued motion, turn into most Kingdoms of the Earth the plenty of abundant Riches that they are commonly fed withall: For Trafique in his right description, is the very soul of a King-dom; and should but Fate ordain a removal of it for some years, from the richest and most popu-lous Monarchy that dwells in the most fertile clyme of the whole Universe, he would soon find by a woful experiment, the miss and loss of so

reviving a supporter. And I am certainly confident, that *England* would as soon feel her feeble-
ness by withdrawment of so great an upholder;
as well in reference to the internal and healthful
preservative of her Inhabitants, for want of those
Medicinal Drugs that are landed upon her Coast
every year, as the external profits, Glory and
beneficial Graces that accrue by her.

Paracelsus might knock down his Forge, if Trafique and Commerce should once cease, and grynde
the hilt of his Sword into Powder, and take some
of the Infusion to make him so valorous, that he
might cut his own Throat in the honor of *Mercury :*
Galen might then burn his Herbal, and like *Joseph
of Arimathea*, build him a Tomb in his Garden,
and so rest from his labours: Our Physical Collegians of *London* would have no cause then to
thunder Fire-balls at *Nich. Culpeppers* Dispensatory:* All Herbs, Roots, and Medicines would

---

* Nicholas Culpeper was a writer on astrology and medicine.
" In 1649 Culpeper brought himself into wider note by publishing
an English translation of the college of Physicians' ' Pharmacopœia '
under the title of ' A Physical Directory, or a Translation of the
London Dispensatory.' . . . This unauthorized translation ex-
cited the indignation of the college of Physicians, which was reflected
in the royalist periodical ' Mercurius Pragmaticus.' . . . The
book is there described as ' done (very filthily) into English by one
Nicholas Culpeper, who commenced the several degrees of Inde-
pendency, Brownism, Anabaptism; admitted himself of John Good-
win's school (of all ungodliness) in Coleman Street; after that he
turned Seeker, Manifestarian, and now he is arrived at the battle-
ment of an absolute Atheist, and by two years drunken labor hath
Gallimawfred the apothecaries book into nonsense, mixing every
receipt therein with some scruple, at least, of rebellion or atheism,

bear their original christening, that the ignorant might understand them: *Album grecum* would not be *Album grecum* then, but a Dogs turd would be a Dogs turd in plain terms, in spight of their teeth.

If Trade should once cease, the Custom-house would soon miss her hundreds and thousands Hogs-heads of Tobacco,* that use to be throng in her every year, as well as the Grocers would in their Ware-houses and Boxes, the Gentry and Commonalty in their Pipes, the Physician in his Drugs and Medicinal Compositions: The (leering) Waiters for want of imployment, might (like so many *Diogenes*) intomb themselves in their empty Casks, and rouling themselves off the Key into the *Thames*, there wander up and down from tide to tide in contemplation of *Aristotles* unresolved curiosity, until the rottenness of their circular habitation give them a *Quietus est*, and fairly surrender them up into the custody of those who

besides the danger of poisoning men's bodies. And (to supply his drunkenness and leachery with a thirty shilling reward) endeavored to bring into obloquy the famous societies of apothecaries and chyrurgeons.' The translation has none of the defects here attributed to it and the abuse was obviously inspired by political opponents and the societies whose monopolies Culpeper was charged with having infringed."— *Dictionary of National Biography*.

* England was at this time levying an import duty of twopence per pound on this commodity, and early in the next century the amount received annually from Maryland exceeded twenty-five thousand hogsheads, of which the average weight was at least eight hundred pounds. The census of 1900 gives 24,589,480 pounds as the tobacco crop of Maryland of to-day.

both for profession, disposition and nature, lay as near claim to them, as if they both tumbled in one belly, and for name they jump alike, being according to the original translation both *Sharkes.*

Silks and Cambricks, and Lawns to make sleeves, would be as soon miss'd at Court, as Gold and Silver would be in the Mint and Pockets: The Low-Country Soldier would be at a cold stand for Outlandish Furrs to make him Muffs, to keep his ten similitudes warm in the Winter, as well as the Furrier for want of Skins to uphold his Trade.

Should Commerce once cease, there is no Country in the habitable world but would undoubtedly miss that flourishing, splendid and rich gallantry of Equipage, that Trafique maintained and drest her up in, before she received that fatal Eclipse: *England, France, Germany* and *Spain*, together with all the Kingdoms ——

But stop (good Muse) lest I should, like the Parson of *Pancras*, run so far from my Text in half an hour, that a two hours trot back again would hardly fetch it up: I had best while I am alive in my Doctrine, to think again of *Mary-Land*, lest the business of other Countries take up so much room in my brain, that I forget and bury her in oblivion.

The three main Commodities this Country affords for Trafique, are Tobacco, Furrs, and

Flesh. Furrs and Skins, as Beavers, Otters, Musk-Rats, Rackoons, Wild-Cats, and Elke or Buffeloe, with divers others, which were first made vendible by the *Indians* of the Country, and sold to the Inhabitant, and by them to the Merchant, and so transported into *England* and other places where it becomes most commodious.

Tobacco is the only solid Staple Commodity of this Province: The use of it was first found out by the *Indians* many Ages agoe, and transferr'd into Christendom by that great Discoverer of *America Columbus.* It's generally made by all the Inhabitants of this Province, and between the months of *March* and *April* they sow the seed (which is much smaller then Mustard-seed) in small beds and patches digg'd up and made so by art, and about *May* the Plants commonly appear green in those beds: In *June* they are transplanted from their beds, and set in little hillocks in distant rowes, dug up for the same purpose; some twice or thrice they are weeded, and succoured from their illegitimate Leaves that would be peeping out from the body of the Stalk. They top the several Plants as they find occasion in their predominating rankness: About the middle of *September* they cut the Tobacco down, and carry it into houses, (made for that purpose) to bring it to its purity: And after it has attained, by a convenient attendance upon time, to its perfection, it is then tyed up in bundles, and packt into Hogs-heads, and then laid by for the Trade.

Between *November* and *January* there arrives in this Province Shipping to the number of twenty sail and upwards,* all Merchant-men loaden with Commodities to Trafique and dispose of, trucking with the Planter for Silks, Hollands, Serges, and Broad-clothes, with other necessary Goods, priz'd at such and such rates as shall be judg'd on is fair and legal, for Tobacco at so much the pound, and advantage on both sides considered; the Planter for his work, and the Merchant for adventuring himself and his Commodity into so far a Country: Thus is the Trade on both sides drove on with a fair and honest *Decorum.*

The Inhabitants of this Province are seldom or never put to the affrightment of being robb'd of their money, nor to dirty their Fingers by telling of vast sums: They have more bags to carry Corn, then Coyn; and though they want, but why should I call that a want which is only a necessary miss? the very effects of the dirt of this Province affords as great a profit to the general Inhabitant, as the Gold of *Peru* doth to the straight-breecht Commonalty of the *Spaniard.*†

---

* By the middle of the next century about fifty vessels were owned by the inhabitants of the province.

† In the year 1729 the governor of the province had a decidedly different opinion, for in that year he wrote: " When our tobacco is sold at home, whatever is the product, it returns to us not in money,

Our Shops and Exchanges of *Mary-Land*, are the Merchants Store-houses, where with few words and protestations Goods are bought and delivered; not like those Shop-keepers Boys in *London*, that continually cry, *What do ye lack Sir?* *What d'ye buy?* yelping with so wide a mouth, as if some Apothecary had hired their mouths to stand open to catch Gnats and Vagabond Flyes in.

Tobacco is the currant Coyn of *Mary-Land*, and will sooner purchase Commodities from the Merchant, then money.* I must confess the *New-England* men that trade into this Province, had rather have fat Pork for their Goods, then Tobacco or Furrs,† which I conceive is, because their bodies being fast bound up with the cords of restringent Zeal, they are fain to make use of the lineaments of this *Non-Canaanite* creature physically to loosen them; for a bit of a pound upon a two-peny Rye loaf, according to the original

but is either converted into apparel, tools, or other conveniences of life, or else remains there as it were dead to us; for where the staple of a country upon foreign sales yields no return of money to circulate in such a country, the want of such a circulation must leave it almost inanimate: it is like a dead palsie on the public."—*Calvert Papers*, No. 2, p. 69, *et seq.*

* Tobacco, with the exception of a little Spanish and copper coin, was almost the sole currency of the province until the year 1733, when ninety thousand pounds in paper was issued. Fifteen years later the credit of this became good, more such issues followed, and by the close of the colonial era tobacco, as a currency, was nearly displaced by paper.

† A century later New England's chief import from Maryland was grain.

Receipt, will bring the costiv'st red-ear'd Zealot
in some three hours time to a fine stool, if method-
ically observed.

*Medera-*Wines, Sugars, Salt, Wickar-Chairs,
and Tin Candlesticks, is the most of the Commodities they bring in: They arrive in *Mary-Land*
about *September*, being most of them Ketches and
Barkes, and such small Vessels, and those dispers-
ing themselves into several small Creeks of this
Province, to sell and dispose of their Commodities,
where they know the Market is most fit for their
small Adventures.

Barbadoes, together with the several adjacent
Islands, has much Provision yearly from this
Province: And though these Sun-burnt *Phaetons*
think to outvye *Mary-Land* in their Silks and
Puffs, daily speaking against her whom their
necessities makes them beholding to, and like so
many *Don Diegos* that becackt *Pauls*, cock their
Felts and look big upon't; yet if a man could go
down into their infernals, and see how it fares
with them there, I believe he would hardly find
any other Spirit to buoy them up, then the ill-
visaged Ghost of want, that continually wanders
from gut to gut to feed upon the undigested
rynes of Potatoes.

Trafique is Earth's great Atlas, *that supports*
The pay of Armies, and the height of Courts,

And makes *Mechanicks* live, that else would die
Meer starving *Martyrs* to their penury:
None but the *Merchant* of this thing can boast,
He, like the *Bee*, comes loaden from each *Coast*,
And to all *Kingdoms*, as within a *Hive*,
Stows up those *Riches* that doth make them thrive:
Be thrifty, **Mary-Land**, keep what thou hast in store,
And each years *Trafique* to thy self get more.

A Relation of the Customs, Manners, Absurdities, and Religion of the Susquehanock Indians *in and near* Mary-Land.*

A S the diversities of Languages (since *Babels* confusion) has made the distinction between people and people, in this Christendompart of the world; so are they distinguished Nation from Nation, by the diversities and confusion of their Speech and Languages here in *America:* And as every Nation differs in their Laws, Manners and Customs, in *Europe, Asia* and *Africa,* so do they the very same here; That it would be a most intricate and laborious trouble, to run (with a description) through the several Nations of *Indians* here in *America,* considering the innumerableness and diversities of them that dwell on this vast and unmeasured Continent: But rather then I'le be altogether silent, I shall do like the Painter in the Comedy, who being to limne out the Pourtraiture of the Furies, as they severally appeared, set himself behind a Pillar, and between fright and amazement, drew them by guess. Those *Indians*

---

*It was with these Indians (also called Minqua, Andastés, or Gandastogués and Conestogas) that Maryland had most to do. Because of their fear of them the Yaocomicos, in 1634, welcomed the arrival of Lord Baltimore's colonists, and readily gave up their land to them as they were about to seek a safer home elsewhere. Then, after the Susquehannas had given the Maryland colonists only a little trouble, they joined with them in treaties of mutual assistance and defense against the Senecas, Cayugas, and others.

that I have convers'd withall here in this Province
of *Mary-Land*, and have had any occular experimental view of either of their Customs, Manners,
Religions, and Absurdities, are called by the name
of *Susquehanocks*, being a people lookt upon by the
Christian Inhabitants, as the most Noble and
Heroick Nation of *Indians* that dwell upon the
confines of *America;* also are so allowed and lookt
upon by the rest of the *Indians*, by a submissive
and tributary acknowledgement; being a people
cast into the mould of a most large and Warlike
deportment, the men being for the most part seven
foot high in latitude, and in magnitude and bulk
suitable to so high a pitch; their voyce large and
hollow, as ascending out of a Cave, their gate and
behavior strait, stately and majestick, treading
on the Earth with as much pride, contempt, and
disdain to so sordid a Center, as can be imagined
from a creature derived from the same mould and
Earth.

Their bodies are cloth'd with no other Armour
to defend them from the nipping frosts of a be-
numbing Winter, or the penetrating and scorching
influence of the Sun in a hot Summer, then what
Nature gave them when they parted with the dark
receptacle of their mothers womb. They go Men,
Women and Children, all naked, only where
shame leads them by a natural instinct to be
reservedly modest, there they become cover'd.

The formality of *Jezabels* artificial Glory is much courted and followed by these *Indians*, only in matter of colours (I conceive) they differ.

The *Indians* paint upon their faces one stroke of red, another of green, another of white, and another of black, so that when they have accomplished the Equipage of their Countenance in this trim, they are the only Hieroglyphicks and Representatives of the Furies. Their skins are naturally white, but altered from their originals by the several dyings of Roots and Barks, that they prepare and make useful to metamorphize their hydes into a dark Cinamon brown. The hair of their head is black, long and harsh, but where Nature hath appointed the situation of it any where else, they divert it (by an antient custom) from its growth, by pulling it up hair by hair by the root in its primitive appearance. Several of them wear divers impressions on their breasts and armes, as the picture of the Devil, Bears, Tigers, and Panthers, which are imprinted on their several lineaments with much difficulty and pain, with an irrevocable determination of its abiding there: And this they count a badge of Heroick Valour, and the only Ornament due to their *Heroes.*

These *Susquehanock Indians* are for the most part great Warriours, and seldom sleep one Summer in the quiet armes of a peaceable Rest, but keep (by their present Power, as well as by their former Conquest) the several Nations of *Indians* round about them, in a forceable obedience and subjection.

Their Government is wrapt up in so various and intricate a Laborynth, that the speculativ'st Artist in the whole World, with his artificial and natural Opticks, cannot see into the rule or sway of these *Indians*, to distinguish what name of Government to call them by; though *Purchas* * in his *Peregrination* between *London* and *Essex*, (which he calls the whole World) will undertake (forsooth) to make a Monarchy of them, but if he had said Anarchy, his word would have pass'd with a better belief. All that ever I could observe in them as to this matter is, that he that is most cruelly Valorous, is accounted the most Noble: Here is very seldom any creeping from a Country Farm, into a Courtly Gallantry, by a sum of money; nor feeing the Heralds to put Daggers and Pistols into their Armes, to make the ignorant believe that they are lineally descended from the house of the Wars and Conquests; he that fights best carries it here.

When they determine to go upon some Design that will and doth require a Consideration, some six of them get into a corner, and sit in Juncto; and if thought fit, their business is made popular,

---

* Alsop was not competent to criticise Purchas whose volumes are highly prized by students of our early history.

and immediately put into action; if not, they make a full stop to it, and are silently reserv'd.

The Warlike Equipage they put themselves in when they prepare for *Belona's* March, is with their faces, armes, and breasts confusedly painted, their hair greazed with Bears oyl, and stuck thick with Swans Feathers, with a wreath or Diadem of black and white Beads upon their heads, a small Hatchet, instead of a Cymetre, stuck in their girts behind them, and either with Guns, or Bows and Arrows. In this posture and dress they march out from their Fort, or dwelling, to the number of Forty in a Troop, singing (or rather howling out) the Decades or Warlike exploits of their Ancestors, ranging the wide Woods untill their fury has met with an Enemy worthy of their Revenge. What Prisoners fall into their hands by the destiny of War, they treat them very civilly while they remain with them abroad, but when they once return homewards, they then begin to dress them in the habit for death, putting on their heads and armes wreaths of Beads, greazing their hair with fat, some going before, and the rest behind, at equal distance from their Prisoners, bellowing in a strange and confused manner, which is a true presage and fore-runner of destruction to their then conquered Enemy.

In this manner of march they continue till they have brought them to their Barken City, where they deliver them up to those that in cruelty will execute them, without either the legal Judgement of a Council of War, or the benefit of their Clergy at the Common Law. The common and usual deaths they put their Prisoners to, is to bind them to stakes, making a fire some distance from them; then one or other of them, whose Genius delights in the art of Paganish dissection, with a sharp knife or flint cuts the Cutis or outermost skin of the brow so deep, untill their nails, or rather Talons, can fasten themselves firm and secure in, then (with a most rigid jerk) disrobeth the head of skin and hair at one pull, leaving the skull almost as bare as those Monumental Skelitons at Chyrurgions-Hall; but for fear they should get cold by leaving so warm and customary a Cap off, they immediately apply to the skull a Cataplasm of hot Embers to keep their Pericranium warm. While they are thus acting this cruelty on their heads, several others are preparing pieces of Iron, and barrels of old Guns, which they make red hot, to sear each part and lineament of their bodies, which they perform and act in a most cruel and barbarous manner: And while they are thus in the midst of their torments and execrable usage, some tearing their skin and hair of their head off by violence, others searing their bodies with hot irons, some are cutting their flesh off, and eating it before their eyes raw while they are alive; yet all this and much more never makes them lower the Top-gallant sail of their Heroick courage, to beg with a submissive Repentance any indulgent favour from their persecuting Enemies; but with an undaunted contempt to their cruelty, eye it with so slight and mean a respect, as if it were below them to value what they did, they courageously (while breath doth libertize them) sing the summary of their Warlike Atchievements.

Now after this cruelty has brought their tormented lives to a period, they immediately fall to butchering of them into parts, distributing the several pieces amongst the Sons of War, to intomb the ruines of their deceased Conquest in no other Sepulchre then their unsanctified maws; which they with more appetite and desire do eat and digest, then if the best of foods should court their stomachs to participate of the most restorative Banquet. Yet though they now and then feed upon the Carkesses of their Enemies, this is not a common dyet, but only a particular dish for the better sort; for there is not a Beast that runs in the Woods of *America*, but if they can by any means come at him, without any scruple of Conscience they'le fall too (without saying Grace) with a devouring greediness.

As for their Religion, together with their Rites and Ceremonies, they are so absurd and ridiculous, that its almost a sin to name them. They

own no other Deity then the Devil, (solid or pro-
found) but with a kind of a wilde imaginary
conjecture, they suppose from their groundless
conceits, that the World had a Maker, but where
he is that made it, or whether he be living to this
day, they know not. The Devil, as I said before,
is all the God they own or worship; and that
more out of a slavish fear then any real Reverence
to his Infernal or Diabolical greatness, he forcing
them to their Obedience by his rough and rigid
dealing with them, often appearing visibly among
them to their terrour, bastinadoing them (with
cruel menaces) even unto death, and burning
their Fields of Corn and houses, that the relation
thereof makes them tremble themselves when they
tell it.

Once in four years they Sacrifice a Childe to
him, in an acknowledgement of their firm obedience to all his Devillish powers, and Hellish
commands. The Priests to whom they apply
themselves in matters of importance and greatest
distress, are like those that attended upon the
Oracle at *Delphos,* who by their Magic-spells could
command a *pro* or *con* from the Devil when they
pleas'd. These *Indians* oft-times raise great Tem-
pests when they have any weighty matter or
design in hand, and by blustering storms inquire
of their Infernal God (the Devil) *How matters shall
go with them either in publick or private.*

When any among them depart this life, they give him no other intombment, then to set him upright upon his breech in a hole dug in the Earth some five foot long, and three foot deep, covered over with the Bark of Trees Arch-wise, with his face Du-West, only leaving a hole half a foot square open. They dress him in the same Equipage and Gallantry that he used to be trim'd in when he was alive, and so bury him (if a Soldier) with his Bows, Arrows, and Target, together with all the rest of his implements and weapons of War, with a Kettle of Broth, and Corn standing before him, lest he should meet with bad quarters in his way. His Kinred and Relations follow him to the Grave, sheath'd in Bear skins for close mourning, with the tayl droyling on the ground, in imitation of our *English* Solemners, that think there's nothing like a tayl a Degree in length, to follow the dead Corpse to the Grave with. Here if that snuffling Prolocutor, that waits upon the dead Monuments of the Tombs at *Westminster*, with his white Rod were there, he might walk from Tomb to Tomb with his, *Here lies the Duke of* Ferrara *and his Dutchess*, and never find any decaying vacation, unless it were in the moldering Consumption of his own Lungs. They bury all within the wall or Pallisado'd impalement of their City, or *Connadago* as they call it. Their houses are low and long, built with the Bark of

Trees Arch-wise, standing thick and confusedly together. They are situated a hundred and odd miles distant from the Christian Plantations of *Mary-Land*, at the head of a River that runs into the Bay of *Chæsapike*, called by their own name *The Susquehanock River*, where they remain and inhabit most part of the Summer time, and seldom remove far from it, unless it be to subdue any Forreign Rebellion.

About *November* the best Hunters draw off to several remote places of the Woods, where they know the Deer, Bear, and Elke useth; there they build them several Cottages, which they call their Winter-quarter, where they remain for the space of three months, untill they have killed up a sufficiency of Provisions to supply their Families with in the Summer.

The Women are the Butchers, Cooks, and Tillers of the ground, the Men think it below the honour of a Masculine, to stoop to any thing but that which their Gun, or Bow and Arrows can command. The Men kill the several Beasts which they meet withall in the Woods, and the Women are the Pack horses to fetch it in upon their backs, fleying and dressing the hydes, (as well as the flesh for provision) to make them fit for Trading, and which are brought down to the *English* at several seasons in the year, to truck and dispose of them for course Blankets, Guns, Powder, and

Lead, Beads, small Looking-glasses, Knives, and Razors.

I never observed all the while I was amongst these naked *Indians*, that ever the Women wore the Breeches, or dared either in look or action predominate over the Men. They are very constant to their Wives; and let this be spoken to their Heathenish praise, that did they not alter their bodies by their dyings, paintings, and cutting themselves, marring those Excellencies that Nature bestowed upon them in their original conceptions and birth, there would be as amiable beauties amongst them, as any *Alexandria* could afford, when *Mark Anthony* and *Cleopatra* dwelt there together. Their Marriages are short and authentique; for after 'tis resolv'd upon by both parties, the Woman sends her intended Husband a Kettle of boyl'd Venison, or Bear; and he returns in lieu thereof Beaver or Otters Skins, and so their Nuptial Rites are concluded without other Ceremony.

Before I bring my Heathenish Story to a period, I have one thing worthy your observation: For as our Grammar Rules have it, *Non decet quenquam mingere currentem aut mandantem:* It doth not become any man to piss running or eating. These **Pagan** men naturally observe the same Rule; for they are so far from running, that like a Hare, they squat to the ground as low as they can, while the

Women stand bolt upright with their armes a Kimbo, performing the same action, in so confident and obscene a posture, as if they had taken their Degrees of Entrance at *Venice*, and commenced Bawds of Art at *Legorne*.

*A Collection of some Letters that were written by the
same Author, most of them in the
time of his Servitude.*

To my much Honored Friend **Mr. T. B.**

SIR,

I Have lived with sorrow to see the Anointed of
the Lord tore from his Throne by the hands
of Paricides, and in contempt haled, in the view
of God, Angels and Men, upon a public Theatre,
and there murthered. I have seen the sacred
Temple of the Almighty, in scorn by Schismaticks
made the Receptacle of Theeves and Robbers; and
those Religious Prayers, that in devotion Evening
and Morning were offered up as a Sacrifice to our
God, rent by Sacrilegious hands, and made no
other use of, then sold to Brothel-houses to light
Tobacco with.

Who then can stay, or will, to see things of so
great weight steer'd by such barbarous Hounds as
these: First, were there an *Egypt* to go down to,
I would involve my Liberty to them, upon condition ne'er more to see my Country. What? live
in silence under the sway of such base actions, is
to give consent; and though the lowness of my
present Estate and Condition, with the hazard I
put my future dayes upon, might plead a just
excuse for me to stay at home; but Heavens

forbid: I'le rather serve in Chains, and draw the
Plough with Animals, till death shall stop and
say, *It is enough.* Sir, if you stay behind, I wish
you well: I am bound for *Mary-Land,* this day I
have made some entrance into my intended voyage, and when I have done more, you shall know
of it. I have here inclosed what you of me
desired, but truly trouble, discontent and business, have so amazed my senses, that what to
write, or where to write, I conceive my self almost
as uncapable as he that never did write. What
you'le find will be *Ex tempore,* without the use of
premeditation; and though there may want something of a flourishing stile to dress them forth,
yet I'm certain there wants nothing of truth, will,
and desire.

Heavens bright Lamp, shine forth some of thy Light,
But just so long to paint this dismal Night;
Then draw thy beams, and hide thy glorious face,
From the dark sable actions of this place;
Leaving these lustful Sodomites *groping still,*
To satisfie each dark unsatiate will,
Untill at length the crimes that they commit,
May sink them down to Hells Infernal pit.
Base and degenerate Earth, how dost thou lye,
That all that pass hiss, at thy Treachery?
Thou which couldst boast once of thy King and Crown,
By base Mechanicks now art tumbled down,
Brewers *and* Coblers, *that have scarce an Eye,*

Walk hand in hand in thy Supremacy;
And all those Courts where Majesty did Throne,
Are now the Seats for Oliver and Joan:
Persons of Honour, which did before inherit
Their glorious Titles from deserved merit,
Are all grown silent, and with wonder gaze,
To view such Slaves drest in their Courtly rayes;
To see a Drayman that knows nought but Yeast,
Set in a Throne like Babylons red Beast,
While heaps of Parasites do idolize
This red-nos'd Bell, with fawning Sacrifice.
What can we say? our King they've Murthered,
And those well born, are basely buried:
Nobles are slain, and Royalists in each street
Are scorn'd, and kick'd by most men that they meet:
Religion's banisht, and Heresie survives,
And none but Conventicks in this Age thrives.
Oh could those Romans from their Ashes rise,
That liv'd in Nero's time: Oh how their cries
Would our perfidious Island shake, nay rend,
With clamorous screaks unto the Heaven send:
Oh how they'd blush to see our Crimson crimes,
And know the Subjects Authors of these times:
When as the Peasant he shall take his King,
And without cause shall fall a murthering him;
And when that's done, with Pride assume the Chair,
And Nimrod-like, himself to heaven rear;
Command the People, make the Land Obey
His baser will, and swear to what he'l say.

Sure, sure our God has not these evils sent
To please himself, but for mans punishment:
And when he shall from our dark sable Skies
Withdraw these Clouds, and let our Sun arise,
Our dayes will surely then in Glory shine,
Both in our Temporal, and our State divine:
May this come quickly, though I may never see
This glorious day, yet I would sympathie,
And feel a joy run through each vain of blood,
Though Vassalled on t'other side the Floud.
Heavens protect his Sacred Majesty,
From secret Plots, & treacherous Villany.
And that those Slaves that now predominate,
Hang'd and destroy'd may be their best of Fate;
And though Great **Charles** *be distant from his own,*
Heaven I hope will seat him on his Throne.

Vale.

Yours what I may,

G. A.

From the Chimney-corner upon a
low Cricket, where I writ this in
the noise of some six Women,
Aug. 19. *Anno*

To my Honoured Father, at his House.

SIR,

BEfore 1 dare bid Adieu to the old World, or
shake hands with my native Soyl for ever, 1
have a Conscience inwards tells me, that I must

offer up the remains of that Obedience of mine, that lyes close centered within the cave of my Soul, at the Alter, of your paternal Love: And though this Sacrifice of mine may shew something low and thread-bare, (at this time) yet know, That in the Zenith of all actions, Obedience is that great wheel that moves the lesser in their circular motion.

I am now entring for some time to dwell under the Government of *Neptune*, a Monarchy that I was never manured to live under, nor to converse with in his dreadful Aspect, neither do I know how I shall bear with his rough demands; but that God has carried me through those many gusts a shoar, which I have met withall in the several voyages of my life, I hope will Pilot me safely to my desired Port, through the worst of Stormes I shall meet withall at Sea.

We have strange, and yet good news aboard, that he whose vast mind could not be contented with spacious Territories to stretch his insatiate desires on, is (by an Almighty power) banished from his usurped Throne to dwell among the dead. I no sooner heard of it, but my melancholly Muse forced me upon this ensuing Distich.

Poor vaunting Earth, gloss'd with uncertain Pride,
That liv'd in Pomp, yet worse then others dy'd:

Who shall blow forth a Trumpet to thy praise?
Or call thy sable Actions shining Rayes?
Such Lights as those blaze forth the vertues dead,
And make them live, though they are buried.
Thou'rt gone, and to thy memory let be said,
There lies that Oliver *which of old betray'd*
His King and Master, and after did assume,
With swelling Pride, to govern in his room.
Here I'le rest satisfied, Scriptures expound to me,
Tophet *was made for such Supremacy.*

The death of this great Rebel (I hope) will prove an *Omen* to presage destruction on the rest. The World's in a heap of troubles and confusion, and while they are in the midst of their changes and amazes, the best way to give them the bag, is to go out of the World and leave them. I am now bound for *Mary-Land,* and I am told that's a New World, but if it prove no better than this, I shall not get much by my change; but before I'le revoke my Resolution, I am resolv'd to put it to adventure, for I think it can hardly be worse then this is: Thus committing you into the hands of that God that made you, I rest

Your Obedient Son,

G. A.

From aboard a Ship at *Graves-*
end, Sept. 7th. *Anno*

———

To my Brother.

I Leave you very near in the same condition as I am in my self, only here lies the difference, you were bound at Joyners Hall in *London* Apprentice-wise, and I conditionally at Navigators Hall, that now rides at an Anchor at *Gravesend;* I hope you will allow me to live in the largest Mayordom, by reason I am the eldest: None but the main Continent of *America* will serve me for a Corporation to inhabit in now, though I am affraid for all that, that the reins of my Liberty will be something shorter then yours will be in *London:* But as to that, what Destiny has ordered I am resolved with an adventerous Resolution to subscribe to, and with a contented imbracement enjoy it. I would fain have seen you once more in this Old World, before I go into the New, I know you have a chain about your Leg, as well as I have a clog about my Neck: If you can't come, send a line or two, if not, wish me well at least: I have one thing to charge home upon you, and I hope you will take my counsel, That you have alwayes an obedient Respect and Reverence to your aged Parents, that while they live they may have comfort of you, and when that God shall sound a retreat to their lives, that there they may with their gray hairs in joy go down to their Graves.

Thus concluding, wishing you a comfortable

Servitude, a prosperous Life, and the assurance of
a happy departure in the immutable love of him
that made you,   *Vale.*

Your Brother,

G. A.

From *Gravesend, Sept.* 7. *Anno*

To my much Honored Friend **Mr. T. B.** *at his House.*

I Am got ashoar with much ado, and it is very
well it is as it is, for if I had stayed a little
longer, I had certainly been a Creature of the
Water, for I had hardly flesh enough to carry me
to Land, not that I wanted for any thing that the
Ship could afford me in reason: But oh the great
bowls of Pease-porridge that appeared in sight
every day about the hour twelve, ingulfed the
senses of my Appetite so, with the restringent
quality of the Salt Beef, upon the internal Inhabitants of my belly, that a *Galenist* for some dayes
after my arrival, with his Bag-pipes of Physical
operations, could hardly make my Puddings dance
in any methodical order.

But to set by these things that happened unto
me at Sea, I am now upon Land, and there I'le
keep my self if I can, and for four years I am
pretty sure of my restraint; and had I known my
yoak would have been so easie, (as I conceive it
will) I would have been here long before now,
rather then to have dwelt under the pressure of

a Rebellious and Trayterous Government so long as I did. I dwell now by providence in the Province of *Mary-Land*, (under the quiet Government of the Lord *Baltemore*) which Country abounds in a most glorious prosperity and plenty of all things. And though the Infancy of her situation might plead an excuse to those several imperfections, (if she were guilty of any of them) which by scandalous and imaginary conjectures are falsly laid to her charge, and which she values with so little notice or perceivance of discontent, that she hardly alters her visage with a frown, to let them know she is angry with such a Rascality of people, that loves nothing better then their own sottish and abusive acclamations of baseness: To be short, the Country (so far forth as I have seen into it) is incomparable.

Here is a sort of naked Inhabitants, or wilde people, that have for many ages I believe lived here in the Woods of *Mary-Land*, as well as in other parts of the Continent, before e'er it was by the Christian Discoverers found out; being a people strange to behold, as well in their looks, which by confused paintings makes them seem dreadful, as in their sterne and heroick gate and deportments; the Men are mighty tall and big limbed, the Women not altogether so large; they are most of them very well featured, did not their wilde and ridiculous dresses alter their original excellencies: The men are great Warriours and Hunters, the Women ingenious and laborious Housewives.

As to matter of their Worship, they own no other Deity then the Devil, and him more out of a slavish fear, then any real devotion, or willing acknowledgement to his Hellish power. They live in little small Bark-Cottages, in the remote parts of the Woods, killing and slaying the several Animals that they meet withall to make provision of, dressing their several Hydes and Skins to Trafique withall, when a conveniency of Trade presents. I would go on further, but like Doctor *Case,* * when he had not a word more to speak for himself, *I am affraid my beloved I have kept you too long.* Now he that made you save you, *Amen.*

Yours to command,

G. A.

From *Mary-Land, Febr.* 6. *Anno*

And not to forget *Tom Forge* I beseech you, tell him that my Love's the same towards him still, and as firm as it was about the overgrown Tryal, when Judgements upon Judgements, had not I stept in, would have pursued him untill the day of Judgement, *&c.*

---

* John Case, who died in the year 1600, was a writer on Aristotle and a doctor of medicine. He had a high reputation as a disputant and, while engaged in reading logic and philosophy to young men, chiefly Roman Catholics, he wrote and published several handbooks that were for a time popular.

To my Father at his House.

 SIR,

AFter my Obedience (at so great and vast a distance) has humbly saluted you and my good Mother, with the cordialest of my prayers, wishes, and desires to wait upon you, with the very best of their effectual devotion, wishing from the very Center of my Soul your flourishing and well-being here upon Earth, and your glorious and everlasting happiness in the World to come.

These lines (my dear Parents) come from that Son which by an irregular Fate was removed from his Native home, and after a five months dangerous passage, was landed on the remote Continent of *America*, in the Province of *Mary-Land*, where now by providence I reside. To give you the particulars of the several accidents that happened in our Voyage by Sea, it would swell a Journal of some sheets, and therefore too large and tedious for a Letter: I think it therefore necessary to bind up the relation in Octavo, and give it you in short.

We had a blowing and dangerous passage of it, and for some dayes after I arrived, I was an absolute *Copernicus*,* it being one main point of my moral Creed, to believe the World had a pair of long legs, and walked with the burthen of the

---

* At this time there were many who had not yet accepted the Copernican theory.

Creation upon her back. For to tell you the very
truth of it, for some dayes upon Land, after so
long and tossing a passage, I was so giddy that I
could hardly tread an even step; so that all things
both above and below (that was in view) appeared
to me like the *Kentish Britains* to *William the
Conqueror*, in a moving posture.

Those few number of weeks since my arrival,
has given me but little experience to write any
thing large of the Country; only thus much I can
say, and that not from any imaginary conjectures,
but from an occular observation, That this Country of *Mary-Land* abounds in a flourishing variety
of delightful Woods, pleasant Groves, lovely
Springs, together with spacious Navigable Rivers
and Creeks, it being a most healthful and pleasant
situation, so far as my knowledge has yet had
any view in it.

Herds of Deer are as numerous in this Province
of *Mary-Land*, as Cuckolds can be in *London*, only
their horns are not so well drest and tipt with
silver as theirs are.

Here if the Devil had such a Vagary in his head
as he had once among the *Gadareans*, he might
drown a thousand head of Hogs and they'd ne're
be miss'd, for the very Woods of this Province
swarms with them.

The Christian Inhabitant of this Province, as
to the general, lives wonderful well and con-

tented: The Government of this Province is by the loyalness of the people, and loving demeanor of the Proprietor and Governor of the same, kept in a continued peace and unity.

The Servant of this Province, which are stig-matiz'd for Slaves by the clappermouth jaws of the vulgar in *England*, live more like Freemen then the most Mechanick Apprentices in *London*, wanting for nothing that is convenient and neces-sary, and according to their several capacities, are extraordinary well used and respected. So leaving things here as I found them, and lest I should commit Sacriledge upon your more serious meditations, with the Tautologies of a long-winded Letter, I'le subscribe with a heavenly Ejaculation to the God of Mercy to preserve you now and for evermore, *Amen.*

Your Obedient Son,

G. A.

From *Mary-Land, Jan.* 17.   *Anno*

To my much Honored Friend **Mr. M. F.**

SIR,

YOu writ to me when I was at *Gravesend*, (but I had no conveniency to send you an answer till now) enjoyning me, if possible, to give you a just Information by my diligent observance, what thing were best and most profitable to send into this Country for a commodious Trafique.

Sir, The enclosed will demonstrate unto you both particularly and at large, to the full satisfaction of your desire, it being an Invoyce drawn as exact to the business you imployed me upon, as my weak capacity could extend to.

Sir, If you send any Adventure to this Province, let me beg to give you this advice in it; That the Factor whom you imploy be a man of a Brain, otherwise the Planter will go near to make a Skimming-dish of his Skull: I know your Genius can interpret my meaning. The people of this place (whether the saltness of the Ocean gave them any alteration when they went over first, or their continual dwelling under the remote Clyme where they now inhabit, I know not) are a more acute people in general, in matters of Trade and Commerce, then in any other place of the World; and by their crafty and sure bargaining, do often over-reach the raw and unexperienced Merchant. To be short, he that undertakes Merchants imployment for *Mary-Land,* must have more of Knave in him then Fool; he must not be a windling piece of Formality, that will lose his Imployers Goods for Conscience sake; nor a flashy piece of Prodigality, that will give his Merchants fine Hollands, Laces, and Silks, to purchase the benevolence of a Female: But he must be a man of solid confidence, carrying alwayes in his looks the Effigies of an Execution upon Command, if he supposes a baffle or denyal of payment, where a debt for his Imployer is legally due.

Sir, I had like almost to forgot to tell you in what part of the World I am: I dwell by providence Servant to Mr. *Thomas Stocket*, in the County of *Baltemore*, within the Province of *Mary-Land*, under the Government of the Lord *Baltemore*, being a Country abounding with the variety and diversity of all that is or may be rare.   But lest I should Tantalize you with a relation of that which is very unlikely of your enjoying, by reason of that strong Antipathy you have ever had 'gainst Travel, as to your own particular: I'le only tell you, that *Mary-Land* is seated within the large extending armes of *America*, between the Degrees of 36 and 38, being in Longitude from *England* eleven hundred and odd Leagues.

Vale.

G. A.

From *Mary-Land, Jan.* 17. *Anno*

To my Honored Friend Mr. T. B. *at his House.*

SIR,

YOurs I received, wherein I find my self much obliged to you for your good opinion of me, I return you millions of thanks.

Sir, you wish me well, and I pray God as well that those wishes may light upon me, and then I question not but all will do well.   Those Pictures

you sent sewed up in a Pastboard, with a Letter
tacked on the outside, you make no mention at
all what should be done with them: If they are
Saints, unless I knew their names, I could make
no use of them. Pray in your next let me know
what they are, for my fingers itch to be doing
with them one way or another. Our Government
here hath had a small fit of a Rebellious Quoti-
dian, but five Grains of the powder of Subvert-
ment has qualified it.* Pray be larger in your
next how things stand in *England:* I understand
His Majesty is return'd with Honour, and seated
in the hereditary Throne of his Father; God bless
him from Traytors, and the Church from Sacrilegious Schisms, and you as a loyal Subject to the
one, and a true Member to the other; while you
so continue, the God of order, peace and tranquility, bless and preserve you, *Amen.*

Vale.

Your real Friend,

G. A.

From *Mary-Land, Febr.* 20.   *Anno*

To my Honored Father at his House.

SIR,

VVIth a twofold unmeasurable joy I received
your Letter: First, in the consideration
of Gods great Mercy to you in particular, (though

---

* This was the Fendall rebellion. Governor Fendall declared it

weak and aged) yet to give you dayes among the living. Next, that his now most Excellent Majesty *Charles* the Second, is by the omnipotent Providence of God, seated in the Throne of his Father. I hope that God that has placed him there, will give him a heart to praise and magnifie his name for ever, and a hand of just Revenge, to punish the murthering and rebellious Outrages of those Sons of shame and Apostacy, that Usurped the Throne of his Sacred Honour. Near about the time I received your Letter, (or a little before) here sprang up in this Province of *Mary-Land* a kind of pigmie Rebellion: A company of weak-witted men, which thought to have traced the steps of *Oliver* in Rebellion. They began to be mighty stiff and hidebound in their proceedings, clothing themselves with the flashy pretences of future and imaginary honour, and (had they not been suddenly quell'd) they might have done so much mischief (for aught I know) that nothing but utter ruine could have ransomed their headlong follies.

His Majesty appearing in *England*, he quickly (by the splendor of his Rayes) thawed the stiffness of their frozen and slippery intentions. All things

to be his belief that by the Maryland charter King Charles I. had intended to give the freemen, or their deputies, full power to make and enact laws without the lord proprietor's assent. Upon hearing of this the proprietor made his brother Philip governor, and Fendall had not a sufficient following to offer any resistance.

(blessed be God for it) are at peace and unity here now: And as *Luther* being asked once, What he thought of some small Opinions that started up in his time? answered, *That he thought them to be good honest people, exempting their error:* So I judge of these men, That their thoughts were not so bad at first, as their actions would have led them into in process of time.

I have here enclosed sent you something written in haste upon the Kings coming to the enjoyment of his Throne, with a reflection upon the former sad and bad times; I have done them as well as I could, considering all things: If they are not so well as they should be, all I can do is to wish them better for your sakes.   My Obedience to you and my Mother alwayes devoted.

Your Son

G. A.

From *Mary-Land, Febr.* 9.   *Anno*

To my Cosen **Mris. Ellinor Evins.**

E' *re I forget the Zenith of your Love,*

L *et me be banisht from the Thrones above;*

L *ight let me never see, when I grow rude,*

I *ntomb your Love in base Ingratitude:*

N *or may I prosper, but the state*

O *f gaping* **Tantalus** *be my fate;*

R *ather then I should thus preposterous grow,*

E *arth would condemn me to her vaults below.*

V *ertuous and Noble, could my Genius raise*

I *mmortal Anthems to your Vestal praise,*

N *one should be more laborious then I,*

S *aint-like to Canonize you to the Sky.*

The Antimonial Cup (dear Cosen) you sent me,
I had; and as soon as I received it, I went to
work with the Infirmities and Diseases of my
body. At the first draught, it made such havock
among the several humors that had stoln into
my body, that like a Conjurer in a room among a
company of little Devils, they no sooner hear him
begin to speak high words, but away they pack,
and happy is he that can get out first, some up the
Chimney, and the rest down stairs, till they are all
disperst. So those malignant humors of my body,
feeling the operative power, and medicinal virtue of
this Cup, were so amazed at their sudden surprizal,
(being alwayes before battered only by the weak
assaults of some few Emporicks) they stood not
long to dispute, but with joynt consent made their
retreat, some running through the sink of the
Skullery, the rest climbing up my ribs, took my
mouth for a Garret-window, and so leapt out.

Cosen, For this great kindness of yours, in send-
ing me this medicinal vertue, I return you my
thanks : It came in a very good time, when I was
dangerously sick, and by the assistance of God it
hath perfectly recovered me.

I have sent you here a few Furrs, they were all I could get at present, I humbly beg your acceptance of them, as a pledge of my love and thankfulness unto you; I subscribe,

Your loving Cosen,

G. A.

From *Mary-Land, Dec.* 9. *Anno*

To my Brother **P. A.**

Brother,

I Have made a shift to unloose my self from my Collar now as well as you, but I see at present either small pleasure or profit in it: What the futurality of my dayes will bring forth, I know not; For while I was linckt with the Chain of a restraining Servitude, I had all things cared for, and now I have all things to care for my self, which makes me almost to wish my self in for the other four years.

Liberty without money, is like a man opprest with the Gout, every step he puts forward puts him to pain; when on the other side, he that has Coyn with his Liberty, is like the swift Post-Messenger of the Gods, that wears wings at his heels, his motion being swift or slow, as he pleaseth.

I received this year two Caps, the one white, of an honest plain countenance, the other purple, which I conceive to be some antient Monumental

Relique; which of them you sent I know not, and
it was a wonder how I should, for there was no
mention in the Letter, more then, *that my Brother
had sent me a Cap:* They were delivered me in the
company of some Gentlemen that ingaged me to
write a few lines upon the purple one, and because
they were my Friends I could not deny them;
and here I present them to you as they were
written.

Haile from the dead, or from Eternity,
Thou Velvit Relique of Antiquity;
Thou which appear'st here in thy purple hew,
Tell's how the dead within their Tombs do doe;
How those Ghosts fare within each Marble Cell,
Where amongst them for Ages thou didst dwell.
What Brain didst cover there? tell us that we
Upon our knees vayle Hats to honour thee:
And if no honour's due, tell us whose pate
Thou basely coveredst, and we'l joyntly hate:
Let's know his name, that we may shew neglect;
If otherwise, we'l kiss thee with respect.
Say, didst thou cover Noll's *old brazen head,*
Which on the top of Westminster *high Lead*
Stands on a Pole, erected to the sky,
As a grand Trophy to his memory.
From his perfidious skull didst thou fall down,
In a disdain to honour such a crown
With three-pile Velvet? tell me, hadst thou thy fall

From the high top of that Cathedral?
None of the Heroes *of the* Roman *stem,*
Wore ever such a fashion'd Diadem,
Didst thou speak Turkish *in thy unknown dress,*
Thou'dst cover Great Mogull, *and no man less;*
But in thy make methinks thou'rt too too scant,
To be so great a Monarch's Turberant.
The Jews *by* Moses *swear, they never knew*
E're such a Cap drest up in Hebrew:
Nor the strict Order of the Romish *See,*
Wears any Cap that looks so base as thee;
His Holiness hates thy Lowness, and instead,
Wears Peters *spired Steeple on his head:*
The Cardinals descent is much more flat,
For want of name, baptized is A Hat;
Through each strict Order has my fancy ran,
Both Ambrose, Austin, *and the* Franciscan,
Where I beheld rich Images of the dead,
Yet scarce had one a Cap upon his head:
Episcopacy *wears Caps, but not like thee,*
Though several shap'd, with much diversity:
'Twere best I think I presently should gang
To Edenburghs *strict* Presbyterian;
But Caps they've none, their ears being made so large,
Serves them to turn it like a Garnesey *Barge;*
Those keep their skulls warm against North-west gusts,
When they in Pulpit do poor Calvin *curse.*
Thou art not Fortunatus, *for I daily see,*
That which I wish is farthest off from me:

Thy low-built state none ever did advance,
To christen thee the Cap of Maintenance;
Then till I know from whence thou didst derive,
Thou shalt be call'd, the Cap of Fugitive.

You writ to me this year to send you some
Smoak; at that instant it made me wonder that a
man of a rational Soul, having both his eyes
(blessed be God) should make so unreasonable a
demand, when he that has but one eye, nay he
which has never a one, and is fain to make use of
an Animal conductive for his optick guidance,
cannot endure the prejudice that Smoak brings
with it: But since you are resolv'd upon it, I'le
dispute it no further.

I have sent you that which will make Smoak,
(namely Tobacco) though the Funk it self is so
slippery that I could not send it, yet I have sent
you the Substance from whence the Smoak
derives: What use you imploy it to I know not,
nor will I be too importunate to know; yet let me
tell you this, That if you burn it in a room to
affright the Devil from the house, you need not
fear but it will work the same effect, as *Tobyes*
galls did upon the leacherous Fiend.   No more at
present.   *Vale.*

                              Your Brother,
                                    G. A.

From *Mary-Land, Dec.* ii.   *Anno*

To my Honored Friend **Mr. T. B.**

SIR,

THis is the entrance upon my fifth year, and I fear 'twill prove the worst: I have been very much troubled with a throng of unruly Distempers, that have (contrary to my expectation) crouded into the Main-guard of my body, when the drowsie Sentinels of my brain were a sleep. Where they got in I know not, but to my grief and terror I find them predominant: Yet as Doctor *Dunne*, sometimes Dean of St. *Pauls*, said, *That the bodies diseases do but mellow a man for Heaven, and so ferments him in this World, as he shall need no long concoction in the Grave, but hasten to the Resurrection.* And if this were weighed seriously in the Ballance of Religious Reason, the World we dwell in would not seem so inticing and bewitching as it doth.

We are only sent by God of an Errand into this World, and the time that's allotted us for to stay, is only for an Answer. When God my great Master shall in good earnest call me home, which these warnings tell me I have not long to stay, I hope then I shall be able to give him a good account of my Message.

Sir, My weakness gives a stop to my writing, my hand being so shakingly feeble, that I can hardly hold my pen any further then to tell you,

I am yours while I live, which I believe will be but some few minutes.

If this Letter come to you before I'me dead, pray for me, but if I am gone, pray howsoever, for they can do me no harm if they come after me.

Vale.

Your real Friend,

G. A.

From *Mary-Land, Dec.* 13. *Anno*

To my Parents.

FRom the Grave or Receptacle of Death am I raised, and by an omnipotent power made capable of offering once more my Obedience (that lies close cabbined in the inwardmost apartment of my Soul) at the feet of your immutable Loves.

My good Parents, God hath done marvellous things for me, far beyond my deserts, which at best were preposterously sinful, and unsuitable to the sacred will of an Almighty: *But he is merciful, and his mercy endures for ever.* When sinful man has by his Evils and Iniquities pull'd some penetrating Judgment upon his head, and finding himself immediately not able to stand under so great a burthen as Gods smallest stroke of Justice, lowers the Top-gallant sayle of his Pride, and with an humble submissiveness prostrates himself before the Throne of his sacred Mercy, and like those three Lepars that sate at the Gate of *Sama-ria*, resolved, *If we go into the City we shall perish, and if we stay here we shall perish also: Therefore we will throw our selves into the hands of the* Assyrians *and if we perish, we perish:* This was just my condition as to eternal state; my Soul was at a stand in this black storm of affliction: I view'd the World, and all that's pleasure in her, and found her altogether flashy, aiery, and full of notional pretensions, and not one firm place where a distressed Soul could hang his trust on. Next I viewed my self, and there I found, instead of good Works, lively Faith, and Charity, a most horrid neast of condemned Evils, bearing a supreme Prerogative over my internal faculties. You'l say here was little hope of rest in this extreme Eclipse, being in a desperate amaze to see my estate so deplorable: My better Angel urged me to deliver up my aggrievances to the Bench of Gods Mercy, the sure support of all distressed Souls: His Heavenly warning, and inward whispers of the good Spirit I was resolv'd to entertain, and not quench, and throw my self into the armes of a loving God, *If I perish, I perish.* 'Tis beyond wonder to think of the love of God extended to sinful man, that in the deepest distresses or agonies of Affliction, when all other things prove rather hinderances then advantages, even at that time God is ready and steps forth to the support-ment of his drooping Spirit. Truly, about a fort-night before I wrote this Letter, two of our ablest Physicians rendered me up into the hands of God, the universal Doctor of the whole World, and subscribed with a silent acknowledgement, That all their Arts, screw'd up to the very Zenith of Scholastique perfection, were not capable of keeping me from the Grave at that time: But God, the great preserver of Soul and Body, said contrary to the expectation of humane reason, *Arise, take up thy bed and walk.*

I am now (through the help of my Maker) creeping up to my former strength and vigour, and every day I live, I hope I shall, through the assistance of divine Grace, climbe nearer and nearer to my eternal home.

I have received this year three Letters from you, one by Capt. *Conway* Commander of the *Wheat-Sheaf*, the others by a *Bristol* Ship. Having no more at present to trouble you with, but expecting your promise, I remain as ever,

Your dutiful Son,

G. A.

Mary-Land, Apr. 9. *Anno*

I desire my hearty love may be remembered to my Brother, and the rest of my Kinred.

FINIS.